LOOKING BEYOND CREDIT

Business development services and the promotion of innovation among small producers

JONATHAN DAWSON

with

ANDY JEANS

INTERMEDIATE TECHNOLOGY PUBLICATIONS 1997

Published by ITDG Publishing
The Schumacher Centre for Technology and Development
Bourton Hall, Bourton-on-Dunsmore, Rugby, Warwickshire CV23 9QZ, UK
www.itdgpublishing.org.uk

© Intermediate Technology Publications 1997

First published in 1997
Print on demand since 2004

ISBN 1 85339 423 8

All rights reserved. No part of this publication may be reprinted or reproduced or utilized in any form or by any electronic, mechanical, or other means, now known or hereafter invented, including photocopying and recording, or in any information storage or retrieval system, without the written permission of the publishers.

A catalogue record for this book is available from the British Library

ITDG Publishing is the publishing arm of the Intermediate Technology Development Group. Our mission is to build the skills and capacity of people in developing countries through the dissemination of information in all forms, enabling them to improve the quality of their lives and that of future generations.

Typesetting by Diamond People Ltd, Bromyard

Printed in Great Britain by Lightning Source, Milton Keynes

Contents

	Summary	vii
1	Introduction	1
	1.1 Background	1
	1.2 Layout of the paper	2
2	Small producer support and the emergence of minimalist credit	3
3	The effectiveness and impact of minimalist credit: a review of the evidence	5
	3.1 Credit and growth	5
	3.2 Credit and poverty alleviation	6
	3.3 A lack of innovation	6
	3.4 The predominance of trading and processing in lenders' portfolios	7
4	The role of business development services in fostering innovation	9
	4.1 Market saturation	9
	4.2 Other constraints	10
	4.3 The key role of technology: the case of the green revolution	11
	4.4 Liberalization and the growth of market opportunities for small producers	12
	4.5 Summary	12
5	The case studies	14
	5.1 Credit plus programmes	14
	5.1.1 BRAC's Rural Development and Credit Programme – assistance to poultry raisers, Bangladesh	14
	5.1.2 Tinytech Oil Mills, Zimbabwe	16
	5.1.3 Support to alpaca farmers and fibre processors, Bolivia	17
	5.1.4 Rural Enterprise Development Services (REDS), Sarvodaya/ITDG, Sri Lanka	19
	5.2 Training	20
	5.2.1 Training vouchers scheme for microenterprises, Paraguay	20
	5.3 Technology development and dissemination	21
	5.3.1 Technoserve – assistance to palm oil processors, Ghana	21
	5.3.2 Dissemination of the ceramic jiko, Kenya	23
	5.3.3 Treadle pump dissemination, Bangladesh and Senegal	24
	5.4 Networking and support to associations	25
	5.4.1 The FIT programme, Kenya	25
	5.4.2 Assistance to small enterprise associations in Ceara State, Brazil	28
	5.4.3 The Institute of Socio-economic and Technological Research (INSOTEC), Ecuador	29
	5.4.4 Proyectos de Fomento, Chile	30
	5.5 Summary	31

6		Factors underlying high impact and cost-effectiveness in service delivery to small producers	34
	6.1	Achievement of scale of operation	34
		6.1.1 Subsector approach	35
		6.1.2 Working through subsectoral nodal points	36
		6.1.3 Promotion of subcontracting and state procurement	38
		6.1.4 Promotion of programme replication	38
	6.2	Greater role of market mechanisms	38
		6.2.1 Using existing production and marketing channels	38
		6.2.2 Promoting competition between the providers of business development services	39
		6.2.3 Aiming at full financial sustainability for the institutions created by projects	39
		6.2.4 Small producers pay for services	40
	6.3	Facilitative role of the state	40
	6.4	Enhanced exposure of small producers to the outside world	41
	6.5	Summary	42
7		The way forward	43
	7.1	Maximizing synergies between financial and business development services	43
	7.2	Building on recent market-driven developments	44
		7.2.1 Share the risks of motivation	44
		7.2.2 Promote the acquisition of uncodified knowledge	44
		7.2.3 Experiment with clusters and associations	44
		7.2.4 Put decisions on service provision into the hands of the clients	45
		7.2.5 Make the revenue of support agencies dependent on the performance of their clients	45
	7.3	Improving impact monitoring and assessment	45
	7.4	Developing strategies for those areas where market mechanisms are less effective	46
	7.5	Re-examining questions of sustainability and subsidy	46
	7.6	Conclusion	47
		Bibliography	48

Summary

In recent years, minimalist credit – that is, where credit alone is provided – has become the predominant form of support to small producers. In parallel, the role of business development services – the term used to describe all non-financial services – has diminished. The former is regarded as successful in reaching large numbers of people and achieving high rates of cost recovery, while the latter are often dismissed as expensive, limited in their impact, and offering little scope for financial sustainability.

Studies into the developmental impact of minimalist credit schemes find that they are generally beneficial. However, most temper their enthusiasm with two important reservations. First, while there are obvious immediate benefits, these are in many cases neither particularly deep in terms of their impact nor sustainable over time. Second, the poorest often derive few or no benefits and can, in fact, be disadvantages as a result of credit schemes.

The core reason for these limitations is the failure of minimalist credit to effect an upgrading in productive capacity or productivity. Credit tends to be used to increase the scale of existing activities rather than to move into new, more sophisticated or higher value-added areas. Small producers generally face a range of constraints other than finance, including access to improved technology, raw materials, skills training, and information on market opportunities.

Significant achievements are recorded in the case studies presented here in terms of employment generation, increased incomes, product innovation and diversification, import substitution and the building of productive capacity. Their performance measured against three key measures of success– benefit:cost ratio, financial sustainability, and scale of impact – is generally high. These achievements are based on innovations in project design and delivery in two areas.

First, significant scale of impact has been achieved primarily through the adoption of subsector analysis – analysis of the vertical structure of the economic activity concerned. This has permitted the identification of system nodes, where many products or services pass through a small number of hands. This has enabled services to be delivered to and through strategically placed enterprises, traders, and small producer associations and clusters, which are able to provide benefits to large numbers of small producers. Much greater attention to project replication than previously has also contributed to a larger scale of impact being achieved.

Second, considerably greater use is made of market mechanisms than before, both for the delivery of project services and for the dissemination of the benefits generated by projects. Four trends in particular are noticeable:

- using and strengthening existing private sector production and marketing channels rather than seeking to override them;
- promoting competition between the providers of business development services;
- aiming at full financial sustainability for the institutions created by projects; and
- requiring that client small producers pay at least a portion of the cost of services.

The time now appears ripe for a reorientation of policy towards small producer support. The primary concern of those initiating and funding credit programmes in recent years has been with their financial sustainability – that is, that they be able to generate enough revenue to be self-supporting. It is now necessary to set this concern alongside questions of sustainability of impact. Strong and sustainable growth in the small producer sector requires that there be a more complementary approach, with a greater role for targeted business development services.

Credit is certainly a missing bridge on the road to development, and technology is another. But alone, they provide only part of the solution.

Smillie, 1991

1 Introduction

1.1 Background

The poor are still with us – more so today than ever, in fact. Around one-fifth of the world's population lives in absolute poverty and global disparities in wealth are growing. To those with access to capital and technology, the process of globalization promises rich rewards. Those without, in the 'excluded' portion of the world economy, are in danger of being left ever further behind. With the global economy being driven by the needs of industry and consumers in its richer segment, 'the form and direction of technical change is racing off at a trajectory that is further and further away from the needs and capabilities of the "excluded majority" ' (Barnett, 1995).

This is the world with limited access to financial capital, modern technology, and external markets where the dominant form of production is at the micro and small scale. It is where most basic needs – for food, shelter, domestic and production equipment and many services – are met not by the trade-driven global economy, but by local small-scale producers. It is where a growing proportion of the world's population, and especially of its poor, will live.

For several decades, governments and international aid agencies have recognized the importance of directing their attention towards this segment of the economy. Support to small producers[1] has been seen as a key element of policies to alleviate poverty. Furthermore, with small firms demonstrating great dynamism and innovation in the industrialized world, increasing interest has been shown in the small-scale sector as a potential motor of economic growth.

Recent years have seen a significant shift in the nature of support to small producers. Much of this has conventionally taken the form of business development services,[2] such as technology development, marketing assistance, business management training, vocational training, and so on. Such services, however, have largely fallen out of favour in recent years. They have generally come to be seen as expensive, limited in their impact, unsustainable and tending to be supply driven.

Today, the dominant instrument of small producer support has become minimalist credit – that is, where credit is the only service provided. In many respects, this approach has been highly successful. Assistance has been effectively delivered to large numbers of poor, small producers. Moreover, many schemes have been able to generate sufficient revenue to cover a high proportion of their costs, and several may even have achieved full financial sustainability.

Beyond credit?

So can the core problems of small producers now be considered to have been solved? Replication of group-based lending schemes (such as, most famously, that of the Grameen Bank) has enjoyed considerable success. Is the principal function of small producer support henceforth to be limited to the refinement and further replication of such schemes?

This paper argues that this is not enough: that credit on its own, in fact, fails to address many of the constraints faced by small producers. This is not to argue that credit is unimportant in helping the poor to lift themselves out of poverty. Rather, it can be seen as a necessary but not sufficient condition. Indeed, central to the argument here is that the effectiveness and impact of credit schemes are likely to be significantly enhanced if other, complementary tools are available.

---

[1] For the purposes of this paper, 'small producers' refers to all those producing on a small scale, including farmers, food processors, artisans and micro- and small-scale entrepreneurs (MSEs). Small-scale trading enterprises are not covered in this study. No strict definition of MSE is adopted here. However, many of the case studies described in the paper use an upper limit of 10 employees to describe MSEs and this commends itself as a common-sense definition for our purposes.

[2] The term 'business development services', which has gained wide currency in recent debates, will be used when referring to all small producer services other than credit and savings.

The aim then – through a broad trail of relevant literature and the presentation of a number of case studies – is to suggest that credit provision is but one among a number of services that are required by small producers if they are to break out of the cycle of poverty in which they are all too often trapped.

This is decidedly *not* to argue for a return to blueprint, formulaic approaches or to large-scale, integrated packages of assistance, typically delivered by large, inefficient institutions. Any study into business development services must begin with an acknowledgement that to date they have frequently been expensive and limited in their impact. However, as a review of the British government's aid programme's small enterprise activities argued: 'it seems clear that the lesson to be drawn from this is that there is much to be learned about designing, delivering and paying for such services – not that they are unneeded or prohibitively expensive' (Grierson, 1994).

This paper can be seen as a response to that challenge: an attempt to map out the known terrain, as well as that which remains to be explored, in the development of cost-effective,[3] high-impact support services for small producers. Specifically, our aims are fourfold:

1. to describe the limitations of minimalist credit as a strategy for small producer support;
2. to demonstrate the need for business development services, particularly those of a technological nature, if small producers are to enhance their capacity and productivity;
3. to identify the factors underlying high-impact, cost-effective business development services; and
4. to identify ideas and innovations in service design and delivery that are worthy of further exploration.

1.2 Layout of the paper

Chapter 2 briefly reviews the rationale for support to small producers and traces the evolution of minimalist credit as the principal support mechanism currently employed.

Chapter 3 provides an analysis of the available evidence on the impact of minimalist credit programmes.

Chapter 4 identifies binding constraints on small producers other than access to credit and makes the case for a more complementary approach, with an important role for business development services.

Chapter 5 presents case studies of a wide range of projects in Africa, Asia and Latin America which illustrate the potential benefits to be had by looking beyond minimalist credit. These include both projects which adopt a complementary 'credit plus' approach, comprising financial and business development services, and those in which there is no financial component but where there is evidence of interesting innovations in cost-effective, high-impact service delivery.

Chapter 6 examines trends and patterns emerging out of the case studies which underlie the emergence of high-impact, cost-effective business development services.

Finally, Chapter 7 attempts to identify outstanding gaps in our knowledge where further research and project-level experimentation are necessary.

---

[3] The term 'cost-effectiveness' is used in this paper to cover two closely related concepts: first, the ability of a project to deliver given services at the lowest possible cost; and second, value for money – i.e. total benefits exceeding costs. An intervention delivering a service as economically as possible, but where costs far outweighed benefits, would not be considered to be cost-effective.

2 Small producer support and the emergence of minimalist credit

The rationale for support to small producers rests on the premise that the wider social and economic benefits of a well functioning support system will exceed the returns to private producers themselves. Whereas large-scale producers, it is argued, are able unaided to pay for or undertake in-house the acquisition of necessary information, skills and equipment, small producers are necessarily more dependent for these on external sources. However, there exist informational and other market failures associated with the provision of business development services to small producers (Levy et al., 1994).

Among the wider social and economic benefits seen to accrue from a healthy and efficient small producer sector, the following are generally seen as particularly important:

- a positive impact on employment;
- a more equitable distribution of income within countries;
- import substitution;
- a more dynamic, flexible and competitive private sector, with improved domestic linkages of all kinds; and
- enhanced food security.

In view of these potential benefits, it is argued, if governments or other development agencies can intervene in a cost-effective manner to improve the performance of small producers beyond what would be achieved in a wholly private marketplace, they should do so (ibid.).[4]

Following this logic, from the 1950s, governments and international aid agencies subsidized the delivery of services to small farmers and, with the 'discovery' of the informal sector in the early 1970s, similar support was extended to microenterprises. This support took many forms: subsidized credit, technical and technological support services, business and technical training, assistance with identifying and accessing new markets and so on.

The shortcomings of many of these approaches became increasingly evident. Better off and politically more powerful groups were able to use their influence to gain access to the subsidized credit intended for the poor. Many services were offered as a standard, 'blueprint' package, with insufficient consideration of location-specific cultural, social and economic factors. And with scant attention frequently paid to project impact and cost-effectiveness, donors found themselves tied into the long-term funding – often with no exit strategy – of projects whose impact on the poor was uncertain.

The 1980s saw a move towards more market-based approaches. Henceforth, service provision would increasingly be driven by the demands of the target group, and those demands should be expressed in terms of significant beneficiary contributions, sufficient to cover most, if not all, of the costs of service delivery. The subsidizing of services, particularly on a long-term basis, became progressively more difficult to defend.

In this climate, understandable excitement was generated by innovations in the provision of credit facilities to the poor. Contrary to the predictions of many, credit-providing agencies proved able to cover a high proportion of their costs through the use of group lending systems and the achievement of scale by lending to large numbers of people. A small number of schemes may even have achieved full financial sustainability.

---

[4] It is true that among those promoting minimalist credit are some who have no specific interest in small producer support and whose sole concern is the effective functioning of financial markets. This paper is addressed to those who see a role for the state and other actors in the promotion of small producers and who are concerned with finding the most effective mix of financial and business development services.

The providers of business development services have found it progressively more difficult to compete for donor funds in the face of these achievements. In addition to the problems described above, they face a number of problems intrinsic to the nature of the services they provide which makes financial sustainability more difficult to achieve than in the case of credit:

- services often need to be customized to specific areas or types of clients, making scale difficult to attain;
- frequently, impacts are somewhat dispersed, with 'ripple effects' taking the benefits far beyond the immediate target group, making global impact difficult to measure; and
- the overhead and capital costs involved in certain activities, such as training and technology development and dissemination, are often necessarily high.

Furthermore, since in many cases small producers are largely unaware of the potential benefits of new or improved techniques, effective demand for many business development services is often low. Clients are unlikely to make significant contributions to services of whose benefits they are unsure.

Consequently, in recent years business development services have declined in popularity and credit programmes have taken an ever higher proportion of the portfolio of donor projects targeted towards the poor. The new Consultative Group to Assist the Poorest (CGAP), for example, funded by the World Bank and with funding of US$200 million from various sources, is dedicating its entire programme to credit for very small businesses (ibid.).

But just how successful has minimalist credit been in addressing poverty alleviation and stimulating growth? That will be the subject of the next chapter.

3 The effectiveness and impact of minimalist credit: a review of the evidence

Until recently, few evaluations of microcredit schemes have, in fact, attempted to measure the impact of credit programmes at the household, enterprise or subsectoral level. Even now, this is rarely attempted by project implementers. Impact evaluation at these levels has generally been considered to be unnecessarily complicated, time consuming and expensive to achieve. Instead, a number of proxy indicators have been used to measure impact. Those most commonly employed are levels of repayment, the number of borrowers and the subsidy-dependence index (a measure of the sustainability of the financial-service institution) (Yaron, 1992).

However, impact, even in the presence of very high coverage and repayment rates and positive sustainability ratings, cannot be taken for granted. In fact, it has been pointed out that: 'the preference for direct credit programmes has developed despite little evidence of the net impact of these programmes on poverty' (Berger, 1989).

So, what of the recent evidence that is emerging? Most studies into the impact of credit agree that it has a generally benign impact on poverty. Interviews with borrowers record an overwhelmingly favourable reaction from the clients themselves while impact analyses point to increases in income and in employment within the family of the borrower (see, for example, Chen, 1996; Hulme and Mosley, 1996; and MkNelly and Dunford, 1996, for recent cross-country case studies).

Many studies, however, temper their enthusiasm with two serious reservations. First, while there are obvious immediate benefits, these are in many cases neither particularly deep in terms of their impact nor sustainable over time. Second, the poorest often derive few or no benefits and can, in fact, be disadvantaged as a result of credit schemes. Let us examine these two arguments in turn.

3.1 Credit and growth

The finding that the short-term benefits generated by microcredit programmes are often neither strong nor long term in their impact recurs frequently in studies. A study of an agricultural credit project in Gambia, for example, found that while almost all interviewed borrowers were very positive about the benefits of the loans: 'it appeared the resulting increases in yield had not reduced the length of the hungry season and there was no evidence that these improvements had enabled processes of accumulation and expansion of agricultural production to take place over subsequent seasons' (Johnson and Rogaly, 1997).

A USAID review of 32 research and evaluation reports found that while credit can have an important role to play in enabling microenterprises to survive in the face of economic crises, few 'experience sustained growth [while] a majority grow only a little and even out, or maintain their operations at a constant level' (Sebstad and Chen, 1996). This finding is mirrored in another major cross-country study: 'it was unusual for credit to trigger a continuous increase in technical sophistication, output or employment: it was much commoner for each of these variables to reach a plateau after one or two loans and remain in a steady state' (Hulme and Mosley, 1996).

The employment impact of minimalist credit appears to be particularly weak. Hulme and Mosley's (1996) study found that while there had been an increase in employment among the family members of borrowers, employment impacts *outside* the family were small. They concluded that this is a natural result of limited technological change.

Another overview study found that minimalist credit programmes tend to preserve and diversify the self-employment of entrepreneurs rather than create additional employment opportunities for others (Berger, 1989). The USAID study referred to above came to similar conclusions:

> Of the 20 studies which focused on [employment], most found positive but small impacts on the number of paid employees . . . and these impacts were concentrated among a small proportion of the borrowers. These findings indicate that the most significant employment impacts were related to increased use of family labour, or increased hours of work by owners or current workers. It is common for increases in either family or paid employment to reach a plateau after several loans and then remain steady. (Sebstad and Chen, 1996)

3.2 Credit and poverty alleviation

There is also evidence that the poorest have derived little benefit from minimalist credit programmes and even in some cases that they have been disadvantaged by them. The Hulme and Mosley (1996) study concluded that the poorer the borrower, the less was the increase in income from a small loan, and at the bottom end of the scale some of the poorest borrowers became worse off as a result of receiving loans. This point is echoed by a recent study in India which identified strong limits – in terms of skills, technology and marketing opportunities – on the ability of the poorest to absorb credit (Mayoux, 1995). An evaluation of a credit programme for poor women in India found that they were maintaining good repayment rates, but the small profits they made were used primarily to pay the interest due on the loans (Berger and Buvinic, 1989).

One of the obvious ways in which the poorest can lose out as a result of credit schemes is through exclusion from borrower groups: if further loans to group members are conditional on full repayment of outstanding credit, the least able to repay may well be excluded. There is evidence that this has in fact happened. In a credit programme in India, for example, 'whole groups of once-organized women were rendered inactive. These inactive women were clearly the poorer members and had been excluded rather than withdrawn themselves' (Naponen, 1987).

Similarly, in Bangladesh those with no land (a large proportion of the rural poor) have been found to derive little benefit from minimalist credit schemes (Osmani, 1989). In this densely populated setting, imposing a ceiling of half an acre 'to prevent loans being allocated to better-off people does not necessarily mean that the poorest are included' (Rogaly, 1996).

An additional area of concern, in terms of the impact of loans on the poorest, concerns usurpation by men of loans targeted specifically at women. A study into the impact of credit provided by BRAC (Bangladesh Rural Advancement Committee), the Grameen Bank and several other Bangladeshi agencies on women's empowerment found that in 53 per cent of cases women exercised only partial or limited control over loans made in their name. Furthermore, women were found to have greater control over small loans made for purposes which did not challenge the existing gender division of labour (Goetz and Sen Gupta, 1994).

Hulme and Mosley (1996) concluded that: 'the poorest people have little access to these schemes, are likely to take on unreasonable risks if they do participate, and the benefits are most likely to accrue to "middle"- and "upper"-income poor who have crossed an economic threshold that means a major part of their income is secure'.

In summary, the picture to emerge from these recent studies is that minimalist credit may not be as effective in addressing the needs of small producers as has often been supposed. There appears to be a definite ceiling – in many cases a rather low ceiling – on the growth that is stimulated by improved access to credit, with the poorest in particular enjoying few of the benefits.

3.3 A lack of innovation

This can be explained primarily by the fact that minimalist credit tends to have only a marginal impact on technical innovation and productivity. In both the cross-country survey undertaken by Hulme and Mosley (1996) and the USAID review of studies (Sebstad and Chen, 1996), technical innovation among borrowers was found to be limited to a subset of those who had taken multiple loans, and only to a minority within that subset. Much more commonly, loans were used either to increase the scale of existing activities or to diversify into other related fields. Few cases of further specialization and technological *deepening* were identified.[5]

Of the nine case studies examined by Hulme and Mosley, in only one did a majority of borrowers adopt new, enhanced technology (and this was an agricultural credit scheme whose purpose was to facilitate the dissemination of one specific technology). In five of the nine cases, those adopting new technology represented 11 per cent or less of the total.

The USAID review, meanwhile, found that increased incomes among enterprises borrowing from credit schemes (which accounted for only around half of the enterprises in most of the studies, remaining the same or even declining for the others) were found to be associated with increased capacity utilization or lower cost supplies and raw materials rather than improved productivity (Sebstad and Chen, 1996).

This is of central importance. If borrowers use loans only to expand their activities rather than to upgrade their production techniques, improve their productivity or move into new higher-value product and service markets, two necessary outcomes follow. First, the ability of producers to absorb credit becomes progressively weaker; that is, a lack of product innovation leads eventually to market saturation. Second, as the markets of small producers – characterized by low levels of productivity, technology and innovation[6] – become flooded, credit risks becoming an instrument in spreading indebtedness rather than enrichment.

It is important to repeat here that our aim is not to suggest that credit is unimportant, or that it is never the binding constraint on small producers. Our reservations have to do not with credit, but with the minimalist approach. Credit, in short, cannot be assumed to be the only constraint on small producers, particularly in view of the evidence that, on its own, it is rarely able to stimulate qualitative improvements.

3.4 The predominance of trading and processing in lenders' portfolios

One of the principal reasons for the lack of innovation and sustained growth among the clients of minimalist credit schemes is that producers are often poorly represented among them. Commonly, lenders' portfolios are dominated by those involved in trade and in simple food-production and -processing activities, where the scope for innovation and qualitative improvements in techniques is limited.

Only 13 per cent of the borrowers from the schemes run by PRIDE Kenya, for example, are producers (Tanburn, 1993). A review of six large credit schemes also found that a large majority of the borrowers were in the retail and food-processing sectors (quoted in Tendler, 1989). Of the 90 per cent of Grameen Bank loans that were made to women in 1990, over 50 per cent were for three traditional activities: dairy cows, paddy husking and cattle fattening (Smillie, 1991).

Smillie describes the impact of a minimalist credit programme run by CARE in Kenya, almost all of whose clients are traders, in the following terms:

The project has proved that poor women can be good credit risks. They are increasing their incomes and building a savings

---

[5] Hulme and Mosley (1996) also found a correlation between relative wealth and the use of credit for innovation: 'richer beneficiaries ... use credit for capital deepening, which increases their expectations of income and risk at the same time, and poorer beneficiaries ... use credit either for capital widening which involves unchanged risks and income, or even to reduce their capitalization and their risks'.

[6] 'Innovation' in the context of this paper refers to the capacity of small producers to introduce higher-value techniques into their productive process, permitting both improved capacity to adapt to changing market conditions, and the production of higher quality and more remunerative goods. Without such capacity, producers are limited to increases in the *volume* of output and will remain limited to the low-quality, low-income markets to which they currently tend to be restricted.

cushion. But there is little or no value added in what they do, no increase in productivity, no reduced dependence on external sources of supply.... Women borrowers assuredly make the best of their loans, but their endeavours are limited to the narrow confines of the world to which they are generally restricted. That is why so many never get beyond traditional handicrafts, food processing and petty trade.... Without tried investment opportunities based on sound technical information and knowledge (there is a distinction), minimalist credit programmes for women will result in minimal improvements. (Smillie, 1991)

The impact of improved access to credit in the context of limited technical innovation and growing labour force pressures is predictable: a flooding of small producer markets which are characterized by low value-added activities, productivity and incomes. This has emerged in recent years as a major feature of the small producer landscape, a symptom of the inadequate attention paid to technical support for innovation. To quote from the conclusions arrived at by Hulme and Mosley (1996):

So long as ... access to training, new technologies and growing markets is restricted, the capacity for dynamic entrepreneurial behaviour is bound to be restricted also.

Small producers face many constraints other than credit, and these vary at different points and stages of the businesses' growth cycle and also vary by subsector. Moreover, releasing one bottleneck frequently exposes other quite different ones.

The next chapter examines some of these other constraints and argues that business development services, and particularly those which focus on enhancing technological capacity, have a key role to play in stimulating innovation and promoting self-sustaining growth among small producers.

4 The role of business development services in fostering innovation

There do, then, appear to be important limitations on the effectiveness and impact of credit when delivered to small producers without any other complementary services. This may appear to be a somewhat surprising finding, not least because surveys frequently find credit to be the most serious constraint identified by small producers themselves – and it is rarely outside of the top two or three cited constraints.

4.1 Market saturation

It should, however, not be forgotten that the producer himself frequently has only a very partial view of the total environment in which he operates: his position in the subsector often affords a very limited view of the global picture. From this perspective, a World Bank report suggests, 'lack of access to credit is the shortcoming most frequently cited by entrepreneurs, perhaps because it is the most readily identifiable' (Dessing, 1990).

This is well illustrated by a study into the impact of structural adjustment on small enterprises in Ghana (Dawson, 1991). Poor access to credit was much the most frequently quoted constraint on enterprise growth by sampled entrepreneurs. From their perspectives, credit would permit the opening of showrooms, access to cheaper raw materials since they could be purchased in bulk, sufficient working capital to take on larger jobs and a range of other advantages.

A study of the macroeconomic environment, however, made it clear that in most of the markets being served by small producers, demand was at best stagnant and more frequently declining. Furthermore, retrenchment and a lack of formal sector employment opportunities were leading to a flood of new market entrants; the low barriers of entry to small enterprise activities left them highly vulnerable to such flooding. In short, a shrinking cake was being cut into ever smaller slices. In such conditions, access to credit could stimulate the growth of individual enterprises, but only at the cost of displacing others which had been unable to acquire loans.

This is what happened with Grameen Bank loans to women in the rice-husking subsector, which took up 14 per cent of the Bank's loans in 1995. Borrowers' incomes rose as a result of these loans.

> But what was the net income gain to Bangladesh? Bangladesh produces about 25 million tons of paddy per year. So, with or without the Grameen Bank's ... loans, millers and villagers husk 25 million tons of paddy. If Grameen's borrowers are husking more, someone else is husking less. It represents pure displacement. (Haggblade, 1995)

This picture of saturated, low-value markets characterized by falling profit margins for small-scale operators appears with ever-increasing frequency in studies and project reports. Gamser and Almond's (1990) description of maize-milling in southern Africa and the Caribbean, for example, found that: 'in many of these countries, the proliferation of micro-mills has lead to a saturation of the market for this service, with the end result being the inability of many of the mills to operate profitably'.

A review of studies into the impact of structural adjustment on small enterprises found the saturation of low-value markets and a general lack of innovation to be a widely shared theme (Dawson and Oyeyinka, 1993). Stagnant or falling profitability was common among most enterprises in the majority of studies covered by this review, with only relatively modern and sophisticated small firms able to diversify into higher value-added activities.

Dawson's study in Ghana also found anomalies in what entrepreneurs understood by 'access to credit'. Informal credit was readily available in the area covered by the study and a number of small-scale machine shops using sophisticated European machine tools had equipped themselves using only these sources. Pointing to credit access was, in many cases, found to be a plea for state assistance – generally understood to be a grant, rather than a loan which would need to be repaid at commercial rates of interest.

4.2 Other constraints

Just as the importance of credit as a constraint may have been overstated, so there has been a parallel tendency to overlook the importance of a range of other problems faced by small producers. We will look here at only a small portion of the literature on this subject: yet this will be sufficient to demonstrate the naïvety of assuming that credit on its own will generally be able to relieve poverty and generate strong self-sustaining growth among small producers.

A study into the problems faced by small enterprises in Nigeria identified many growth constraints, of which credit was among the least critical (Dawson and Oyeyinka, 1993). The most serious of these were market saturation, declining demand, poor access to raw materials (due to greater exports of primary products under structural adjustment) and increased costs of imported items.

Meagher and Yunusa (1994), also studying the situation in Nigeria, found depressed demand and a lack of product diversification to be much more important constraints than access to credit. Similarly, an analysis of small producer markets in Ghana found that: 'microenterprises are constrained more by a lack of demand than a lack of credit' (Holt and Ribe, 1990).

A GEMINI study identified as the key problems facing women mat-weavers in Niger a decline in the availability of palm leaves and an increase in imports of plastic mats from China as a result of import liberalization. The report concluded that women must be helped to diversify out of mat-weaving (Mead et al., 1990). Similarly, Schmitz found declining availability of raw materials to be the most important constraint on weavers and hammock-makers in Brazil (Schmitz, 1989). Access to affordable raw materials was also found to be among the most serious binding constraints identified in the review of small enterprise studies and projects undertaken by Little, Mazumdar and Page (1987).

Poor access to modern equipment has also featured prominently among the binding constraints identified in small producer studies and projects. The Meagher and Yunusa study referred to above (1994) found that, in the face of sharply increased prices of imported tools and spare parts as a result of the country's structural adjustment programme, one-quarter of sampled small-scale entrepreneurs in Nigeria had fewer operational tools than when the programme was adopted.

Dawson and Oyeyinka also found significant technological downgrading among small producers in Nigeria (1993), while Bagachwa (1991) and Dawson (1993) both found technological investment among small-scale producers in Tanzania to be limited to the relatively rich and well-connected Indian business community. All three of these studies found poor access to modern equipment to be a binding constraint on the ability of small enterprises to respond positively to the fresh market opportunities arising as a result of structural adjustment.

In summary, small producers face a number of important problems other than access to credit. There are unquestionably instances where the provision of credit on its own will release the binding constraint on certain types of small producers. However, this cannot be *assumed* to be the case – and only in certain limited circumstances, in fact, is it likely to be true.

Furthermore, as will be suggested in a number of the case studies in the next chapter, a releasing of the credit bottleneck may well bring to the fore other problems not previously identified which have nothing to do with access to finance. A recent survey of MSEs in Kenya found that while access to credit is perceived to be the principal problem by MSEs that are not experiencing growth, among those that are growing, market access and 'other problems' assume a higher priority (Daniels et al., 1995).

All this is admirably summed up by a World Bank investigation of successful enterprise support mechanisms and interventions:

> Small and medium-sized enterprises operate in a complex environment and confront a diverse array of constraints; it is chimerical to search for a single constraint, common across countries which, once released, will lead to the rapid development of SMEs. Not only is there substantial variation among countries as to which constraint is binding, the release of one constraint is likely to bring to the forefront some other constraint whose inhibiting influence had not previously been evident. (Levy, 1994)

This is self-evident. And yet it runs counter to the thinking underlying minimalist credit, where credit is assumed in every case to be the principal binding constraint facing small producers.

4.3 The key role of technology: the case of the green revolution

Central to the case being made here is the need for interventions which contribute to an enhancement in the technological capacity of small producers. This is because only on the basis of such enhancement can they innovate, improve the quality and value of their products and increase their capacity to respond to changing market conditions.

This is not to argue for the primacy of technology – in terms of the development and dissemination of hardware – over other business development services. If, as suggested in a recent World Bank study,[7] technological capacity is defined in terms of the ability of producers to identify opportunities; to source, install and operate equipment; to apply skills and techniques to the production process; and to respond to changing market conditions, then almost all types of business development services become relevant.

Enhanced technological capacity is important for another, less tangible reason which goes beyond the realm of economics and into the domain of cultural self-expression and self-confidence. The capacity to produce or adapt one's own tools and equipment is essential for the development not just of economies but also of societies. The confidence needed for self-propelled and locally sustainable development can only be built on the foundations of strengthened technological capacity.

By way of illustration, it may be of value at this stage to look at the synergies generated by complementary financial and business development services in the development and dissemination of 'green revolution' technologies. These technologies consist of high-yielding, mostly hybridized seeds of particular food crops, of which the most important are rice, wheat (in Asia) and maize (in Africa), which for maximum yields need to be accompanied by appropriate fertilizer applications and predictable levels of water supply. The technologies are scale-neutral, in that both yields and unit costs per ton of grain are, in principle, the same for small and large farmers.

Green revolution technologies emerged from a major investment in research and development. Small farmers in Asia have benefited considerably more from the new techniques than those in Africa for two main reasons. First, there are much more effective channels for both the regular and timely delivery of necessary inputs, and the storage and marketing of crops. Second, access to small producer credit is more widespread. Several of the credit agencies studied in the Hulme and Mosley cross-country analysis were created for the very purpose of spreading green revolution technologies to the poor, and the authors stress their importance in disseminating the technologies to small farmers in Asia.

This is an excellent example of how technology development and credit, when delivered in a co-ordinated fashion, can promote innovation and stimulate a qualitative

---

[7] Biggs et al.'s (1995) study of technological capabilities defined technology as covering (1) *investment capabilities* – 'the skills and information needed to identify feasible investment projects, locate and purchase suitable ... technologies'; (2) *production capabilities* – 'the skills and knowledge needed for the operation of a [technology]'; and (3) *learning mechanisms* – the skills and knowledge needed to enable producers to 'change over time the levels of investment and production capabilities' in response to changing conditions.

enhancement in the production of small producers.[8] Although the costs of the technological development work involved were high, there is no question that these have been, and continue to be, more than outweighed by the benefits accruing to farmers – large and small – in the developing world. Despite the fact that benefiting farmers have paid relatively few of the direct costs of the research and development work, the wider social and economic benefits are seen to have justified the investment.

Yet, research and development work of this sort for non-farm enterprises, as well as in other fields of smallholder agriculture, is very hard to justify with donors, one of the principal objections being problems of full cost-recovery from beneficiaries. Now, it is undoubtedly true that few if any research activities are likely to be able to generate the scale and spread of benefits of the green revolution. None the less, the principle remains the same and equivalent cost–benefit ratios may well be achievable with technological investment in other fields.

4.4 Liberalization and the growth of market opportunities for small producers

Recent trends towards increased liberalization and structural adjustment have opened up significant new market opportunities for small producers in the developing world. Currency devaluations have led to (often significant) increases in the cost of imported goods of all kinds; the break up of parastatal monopolies in many countries has created further market space which small producers have the potential to penetrate; and the lowering of trade barriers has created many export opportunities, particularly in the field of non-traditional agricultural exports. With large industries frequently characterized by high levels of import dependency, both for their equipment and spares and for their raw materials, the greater reliance of small producers on domestic resources often offers them a competitive advantage in this new marketplace.

There is indeed some evidence that small producers have been able to some degree to exploit these emerging opportunities. Two studies in Ghana, for example, identified significant areas of small enterprise growth and product enhancement under adjustment (Dawson, 1991; Steel and Webster, 1991). Small machine shops, equipped with modern engineering equipment, sprang up and moved into a wide range of new product and service areas: gears and sprockets, with clients including a Yugoslav motorcycle assembly plant; the production and maintenance of the equipment used by the local lumber mills; saw-benches, wood-turning lathes, sprayers and many other items of equipment used by other small producers; and a variety of food-processing machines.

In almost all studies into the impact of liberalization on small producers, however, only a relatively small proportion of sampled producers report increased profits (for a review of this literature, see Dawson and Oyeyinka, 1993). Much more commonly, they find themselves squeezed by increased competition and falling profit margins. Limited technological capabilities consistently emerge as among the most important constraints on small producers' ability to exploit the new market opportunities.

Where small producers have not been able to identify new market opportunities and, crucially, to access the skills and equipment necessary to permit them to exploit those opportunities, a familiar picture emerges of saturated low-skill, low-value, low-income markets. Assistance with technological upgrading may not always be sufficient in itself to permit small producers to diversify into new, higher-value markets. None the less, it is clearly a necessary central element of programmes seeking to promote such advances.

Summary

Let us review the development of our argument thus far. The minimalist credit revolution appeared to offer solutions to many of

---

[8] We recognize that green revolution technologies continue to provoke controversy in certain quarters, with their impact on the environment and on poor farmers in particular called into question. Our aim here is not to enter this debate, but rather to point out the lessons on offer in terms of strategies for stimulating innovation.

the key problems previously experienced with support programmes to small producers: assistance could be targeted directly at the poor; poor people themselves, rather than uninformed outsiders, would decide on how the credit would be used; and sustainability of the credit institutions could be guaranteed through high rates of cost-recovery.

In all these respects, credit has made major breakthroughs and has exceeded the expectations of many. However, in terms of impact and effectiveness it has proved somewhat disappointing. While many have benefited, there is little evidence of a self-sustaining process of accumulation and growth among poor producers. Furthermore, the poorest of the poor have derived little benefit and in some cases appear to have been actively disadvantaged.

A central reason for the relative lack of impact is that there has been little innovation – in terms of the adoption of higher-quality processes or enhanced capacity to adapt to changing market conditions – among the recipients of minimalist credit. Trade and simple processing activities – which offer limited scope for increased productivity and value-added – have dominated borrowers' portfolios and even among producers, little investment has been made in technological enhancement. Borrowers have tended to expand or diversify current activities rather than to innovate and upgrade. This has resulted in the saturation of a relatively small number of simple, low value-added product markets.

More sophisticated and lucrative markets exist that small producers do have the capacity to enter, given appropriate support. Structural adjustment, by rendering imports (often considerably) more expensive and deregulating many domestic markets, has opened up a large number of higher-value product and service niches. The response of small producers to the emerging opportunities has, however, been generally weak. Yet, where appropriate support has been available, small producers have shown a tremendous capacity for innovation and growth. They have been able to make a substantial contribution to the achievement of key social and economic goals, including employment generation, improved incomes and equity, indigenous technological learning and import substitution.

If a strong case is emerging for a more prominent role for business development services in small producer support, what about the reservations expressed above: in terms of their low impact, limited scale of benefits and poor levels of cost-recovery? Should we accept that, while these services may be valuable, there is simply no way that they can be delivered cost-effectively? No: there is a growing body of empirical evidence that contradicts this conventional wisdom. Much work unquestionably remains to be done in developing high-impact, cost-effective business development services. None the less, there are many encouraging developments on the ground, and this is the subject of the next chapter.

Chapter 5 presents case study material from Africa, Asia and Latin America providing examples of successful business development service initiatives in support of small producers. The case studies will permit the identification of factors underlying high impact and cost-recovery in small producer projects, and these will be discussed in Chapter 6. In the final chapter, we will attempt to draw conclusions and lessons concerning the future direction of small producer support and to identify gaps in our knowledge where further research and project experimentation are required.

5 The case studies

This chapter will describe 12 case studies, most of them recent and many still ongoing, which contain interesting innovations in the delivery of business development services. In some instances, these innovations form part of a 'credit plus' approach, where they are delivered together with financial services. These case studies will be presented first.

In other cases, credit forms no part of the package delivered by the support agencies, but there are none the less important implications in terms of cost-effectiveness and scale of impact. These cases will be presented under the following headings: training; technology development and dissemination; and networks and association support. Where a project has delivered more than one of these services, it will be categorized under the core service provided.

The achievements of the case studies in three key areas – scale of impact, financial sustainability and benefits relative to costs – are summarized at the end of this chapter in Table 5 (see page 32).

No claim is made that these case studies constitute in any sense a representative sample of business development service initiatives. Rather, they have been selected on the grounds that each contains interesting new ideas and approaches which appear to have scope for wider exploration and replication: they can be described as being at the forefront of thinking and experimentation on cost-effective service delivery.

Nor do we pretend that they have no problems or weaknesses. Among the most important roles of the innovator is that of making mistakes from which others can learn. Our reasons for focusing primarily on the positive aspects of these initiatives are threefold:

1 to demonstrate that business development services *can* be delivered cost-effectively;

2 to attempt to identify emerging trends in the delivery of services which underpin their growing cost-effectiveness; and

3 to suggest how these trends can be further strengthened and built upon.

As this is a desk-based study, we have had to rely on written accounts of the various initiatives described. We apologize for any inaccuracies or for the omission of more recent developments in any of the case studies.

One final caveat: presented together in one chapter, the case studies inevitably represent something of a 'mixed bag', covering a huge range both of social, economic and geographic environments and of areas of project activity. Furthermore, there are widespread disparities in the levels of impact data they have generated. In view of this, it should be remembered that our aim is in no sense to embark on a rigorous comparative analysis. For our purposes of increasing awareness and stimulating discussion, impressionistic portraits of the type that follow can serve a useful function.

5.1 Credit plus programmes

5.1.1 BRAC's Rural Development and Credit Programme – assistance to poultry raisers, Bangladesh[9]

> BRAC's assistance to poultry raisers – only one of the many subsectors in which it is active – has achieved a large scale of impact and has generated economic benefits far exceeding investment costs. Poor rural households have been the primary beneficiaries.

Project description
BRAC was established in 1972 as an organization to provide relief and rehabilitation services to refugees from the 1971 war of liberation. Since then it has grown into a

---
[9] This case study draws on Malhotra and Santer (1994), Chen (1996) and Khander and Khalily (1996).

multifaceted development agency with more than 11 000 full-time and 20 000 part-time staff. BRAC has come to the conclusion that credit alone is insufficient for producing sustainable changes in the lives of the rural poor. Consequently, it has developed a range of financial and business development services which are tailored to meet the specific needs of producers in each of the subsectors in which it is active. The cornerstone of BRAC's operation is the Rural Development and Credit Programme (RDP). Under this programme, BRAC helps landless people to establish groups and works with them in basic literacy and numeracy training, enterprise support and the establishment of credit and savings facilities.

In general, BRAC seeks enterprise activities that involve low to intermediate technology, can be managed by the poor, provide long-term employment and yield high returns on investment. A special unit, the Rural Enterprise Project Unit, has been established to develop and test ideas for starting and improving rural enterprises. This unit uses a subsector approach[10] to identify key bottlenecks in areas of activity that dominate the economic life of the poor, namely livestock, fisheries, irrigation, poultry raising and sericulture. It then attempts to unblock those bottlenecks through a variety of different interventions.

An RDP study of the poultry subsector identified a number of important bottlenecks to increased productivity and incomes. Low-yield stock emerged as an initial constraint. In response, BRAC provided training to successful poultry farmers in the establishment of hatchery centres, providing them with credit for the purchase of equipment and stock.

A further problem was found to be high mortality rates among chicks due to disease. BRAC collaborated with the Ministry of Agriculture in establishing a vaccination programme. It then identified village women to be trained as paravets, while the government provided syringes and vaccines free. A further bottleneck, a lack of feed appropriate for the high-yielding chicks, was addressed by the provision of assistance in locating and purchasing ingredients and in their preparation into feeding mixes.

As egg production became more widespread, a deficiency in marketing channels became evident. BRAC clients were encouraged to become egg collectors and sellers and a number were provided with loans to enable them to do so. Paravets also act as collectors and sell on to the traders.

Impact and cost-effectiveness
Starting from one village organization, BRAC's poultry raising programme now covers all the areas in which the RDP is active. By the end of 1990, training had been provided to 98 000 household poultry raisers and 9000 paravets; 665 chick raising units had been established, supplying 750 000 chicks annually; and 95 feed merchants as well as 88 egg sellers had been established, each covering 15 to 20 villages in addition to neighbouring urban centres.

Additional impact has been achieved in BRAC's collaboration with the government's Vulnerable Group Development Programme. BRAC loaned women covered by the scheme money to buy day-old chicks, arranged the necessary input supply links and provided training and technical support to teach them to raise the chicks. By 1994, the programme was reaching around 60 000 individuals.

An economic analysis conducted in 1991 showed that for a total investment by BRAC and the Government of Bangladesh of US$471,494, returns amounted to US$2,172,434 – or 360 per cent. This calculation included interest on loans accruing to BRAC, as well as increases in the incomes of paravets, poultry raisers, chick raisers, egg sellers and feed processors. In addition to these quantifiable benefits, one must add the value of improvements in the status of many thousands of rural people, particularly women, positive nutritional impact and the development of savings, borrowing and banking habits. A subsequent study, comparing the profitability of BRAC-assisted raisers with a group of raisers that BRAC did not

---

[10] This subsector approach is discussed in more depth in Chapter 6.

assist, found that the mean income of the former was almost double that of the latter.

5.1.2 Tinytech Oil Mills, Zimbabwe[11]

> Finding domestic production of appropriate rural oil-milling technology in Zimbabwe unfeasible, ITDG is importing plant from India. This is generating substantial benefits to oil-milling businesses, consumers and the wider rural economy alike: a financial analysis has quantified benefits at over $2 million per annum. There is also significant scale of impact: over 16 000 farmers produce seeds for the mills, while tens of thousands of rural households are able to purchase cooking oil. ITDG is now attempting to identify local agents to take over the import of the equipment.

Project description

An analysis of technical enquiries received by the Intermediate Technology Development Group (ITDG) from Africa on food technologies found that on average 45 per cent related to vegetable oil extraction. In response, ITDG undertook a review of available technological options and, through its country offices in Africa began exploring possible interventions. One technology identified as having potential for use in African conditions was the Indian Tinytech oil mill.

A decision was made to pilot the Tinytech in one of ITDG's countries of operation – Zimbabwe. The four existing oil presses in the country served primarily the major urban centres – their products are expensive in the rural areas. An ITDG survey found that around 90 per cent of rural people find commercially produced cooking oil too expensive to buy. An additional reason for choosing Zimbabwe was that liberalization of the agricultural sector – the removal of government controls on the purchase of sunflower seeds and the production of oil and oil cakes – had created substantial market opportunities for small producers.

ITDG identified local project partners and, beginning in 1989, a series of technical trials of the Tinytech mill involving a farmer's co-operative was undertaken. Studies were also conducted into the technology's commercial potential and into likely social and economic benefits accruing both to manufacturers, operators and sunflower farmers and the local population. Several modifications were made to the design of the mill, which both increased its appropriateness to conditions in Zimbabwe and reduced its cost.

A second pilot phase, launched in 1991, involved the allocation to private operators of four Tinytech mills, imported from India, in various locations in the country. While two of these failed to be commercially viable, this was attributed to management failures. They were redirected to new ownership and the subsequent success of all four mills persuaded the project team to proceed to full dissemination.

Studies into the viability of local production of the technology concluded that, while feasible, it could not be achieved at a cost comparable to that of imports. Production of a number of components, including the sunflower processor and various spares have, however, been adopted by local small-scale metalworkers.

A further 25 have since been bought from India, with credit extended to private operators for their purchase. The equipment costs US$5,755 – a much more expensive technology than ITDG generally works with. The decision was made to proceed with the project on the basis of the potential downstream benefits accruing to the users of mills, ITDG's target group, the rural poor.

The project provides an installation and commissioning service for mill owners and a week of training, usually on-site, in both the technical and business management of the technology. A back-up technical service is also provided by ITDG's office in Harare.

Impact and cost-effectiveness

Commercial evaluations of the mills have found them to be profitable. The average return on investment was calculated to be 51 per cent per annum, meaning that total investment costs can be recouped within two years. Furthermore, and of great importance for rural processors, low break-even levels of production give mills the ability to withstand

---

[11] Drawn from Sunga and Whitby (1995), and discussions with project staff.

even sharp fluctuations in availability of sunflower seeds due to adverse weather or price instability. Two mill owners have since bought a second mill and one is in the process of acquiring a third.

Benefits other than those accruing to the mill owners are realized at a number of different levels. First, employment: the mills provide employment to an average of 10 full-time and three part-time workers. The cost of creating a new job is an average of $2,170 which is in line with the equivalent costs of the Social Dimension Fund ($2,089).

Second, income: the average monthly income of mill employees is $414 for a full-time worker and $212 for a part-time worker, comparing favourably with per capita rural incomes of $163. There has also been an increase in agricultural incomes. Some 95 per cent of sunflower seed is produced by small farmers and they have been encouraged by the presence of the mills to increase production. A typical Tinytech mill buys from 650 farmers, purchasing around US$35,000 worth of seed per annum. Countrywide, a total of 16 250 farmers supply seeds to the Tinytech mills every year.

A reduction in transport costs, immediate payment in cash (rather than delayed payment by cheque, requiring additional transport costs to obtain cash) and the ability to sell small amounts in response to short-term liquidity problems are all important benefits to smallholders.

Third, improved availability and cost of vegetable oil: oil produced by the Tinytech mills is the cheapest on the market, selling for an average of 15 per cent cheaper per litre than that of the major commercial producers. Finally, stimulation of rural economic activity: increased employment and incomes have generated increased demand for a range of goods and services in the areas where the mills are based. Additional informal employment has been generated in maintenance and repair work (an average of two full-time jobs annually per mill), fuelwood collection and the gathering of bottles for which the mills pay a fee. There has also been an increase in the use of oil cake in livestock feed, and of oil in soap-making and in bakeries.

The evaluation found net quantified benefits totalling an annual average of $19,750 per mill. Financial analysis quantified total annual benefits accruing from the 25 mills at over US$2 million.

Full real costs for the import, transport, storage and installation of the mills is charged to the owners. ITDG is now looking for a local agent to take over these functions

ITDG's Technical Enquiries Unit has responded to a large number of enquiries provoked by the Zimbabwean experience and exhibitions at various trade fairs have stimulated considerable interest. An investment prospectus relating to the technology has been produced and is distributed to interested parties in Zimbabwe and a video and book are planned.

5.1.3 Support to alpaca farmers and fibre processors, Bolivia[12]

> Interventions are undertaken on various fronts to improve the quality of fibre production, processing and marketing. Incomes have more than doubled for the 1400 farmers who have benefited so far from this very young project, and the processing and marketing institution created by the project is now financially self-sustaining.

Project description
The raising of alpacas for their thick, warm fibre is one of the few commercial activities open to small, isolated communities on the high plateau of Bolivia. However, it has traditionally been hard, unproductive work: with up to 40 per cent mortality rates among young animals as a result of disease; low fertility due to poor nutrition; overgrazing and consequent degradation of pastureland; and low prices earned from entrepreneurs purchasing the fibre.

To attempt to address some of these problems, a local producer organization, the Integrated Association of Camelid Producers (AIGACAA), together with the US-based NGO, Appropriate Technology International

---
[12] Drawn from ATI (1994) and Hyman et al. (1996).

(ATI), launched a support programme, which received funding from UNDP and UNCDF.

This began with an analysis of the 'value chain' – the steps in production, processing and marketing that add value to a particular product. Division of the value chain into each of its component parts permits the identification both of bottlenecks and of interventions which hold potential to reach large numbers of beneficiaries at key points of the chain. Use of this methodology is central to ATI's work with small producers, and indeed previous experience in working with shepherds in Guatemala facilitated the identification of key blockages in the value chain of alpaca fibre.

Five stages in the value chain were identified – fibre production; primary fibre processing; fibre collection; off-farm processing and secondary processing; and marketing – and appropriate interventions were designed to address constraints at each stage. The quality of fibre production was improved through: a breeding programme to introduce higher quality stock; the introduction of inoculations and parasite baths; a $700,000 credit fund to permit farmers to invest in pumps, wells, improved animal health care, fencing to prevent over-grazing and the purchase of improved stock; and the training of herders – many of them women – in improved farm management and animal husbandry.

Primary fibre processing was improved through the introduction of modern shearing equipment; the training of fibre handlers in improving the quality of fleece; and the establishment of a classification system meeting international standards. A for-profit secondary processing and marketing company, COPROCA, was established in early 1995. It has set up 30 fibre collection points and purchased a ten-ton truck to permit collection and delivery of fibre to its two warehouses. It has also acquired sophisticated processing equipment and trained employees in the processing and classification of the end products.

In addition, COPROCA has engaged textile industry experts to undertake in-depth market surveys and identify niche opportunities. It has also established an information system serving the functions of linking AIGACAA with international buyers and providing up-to-date information on market trends.

Impact and cost-effectiveness

There has been a marked increase in the productivity of the alpaca fibre subsector as a result of the project. The condition of pastureland has improved. Mortality rates are down by 47 per cent in adult animals and 30 per cent in calves, and selective breeding has almost eliminated the production of low-value fibre. Average fibre production per animal has increased by 45 per cent, with a 35 per cent increase in meat production.

COPROCA, the fibre processing and marketing outlet, has become one of the principal buyers of raw fibre in Bolivia and buys from both members and non-members of the association. It has motivated other buyers to increase the prices they offer to alpaca farmers. In its first year of operation, it sold over $600,000 of processed fibre. It is in the process of selling 40 per cent of its shares to alpaca farmers and an additional 20 per cent to other private investors.

Some 1400 farmers had benefited from the programme by the end of 1995, with family incomes more than doubling from an average of $300 to an average of $653 – a total annual net benefit to farmers of just under $0.5 million.

COPROCA now covers all of its costs and hopes in the near future to become a profitable venture. In addition, the project has several sources of revenue to offset the cost of the technical services. First, farmers pay a one-time membership fee of $25 to join AIGACAA. With a substantial increase in membership over the last three years, this has been an important source of revenue. In addition, fees charged for the provision of credit cover one-third of the total costs of business development services. Farmers pay for the full costs of veterinary supplies, but not for the veterinary services. AIGACAA is exploring avenues to further increase revenue.

The United Nations recognized the initiative as one of two exemplary projects for the International Year of Poverty Alleviation. With a view to replication of the project approach, ATI has begun to work with animal fibre producers in Nepal and India and has targeted for future investigation several of the newly independent states of the former Soviet Union.

5.1.4 Rural Enterprise Development Services (REDS), Sarvodaya/ITDG, Sri Lanka[13]

> REDS was created primarily to help Sarvodaya's credit programme increase its scale of impact and improve its repayment rates: these were found to be disappointing because of market saturation, and it was hoped that REDS could help improve the technical sophistication and productivity of small producers.

Project description

Sarvodaya is the largest NGO in Sri Lanka and is working on a wide variety of development activities with poor people in over 2500 villages. One of its larger programmes is the Sarvodaya Economic Enterprise Develop-ment Services (SEEDS). Until 1990, this comprised two sections: one (REP) admin- istering microcredit and the other (MTI) providing simple business training.

However, two important problems became evident. First, repayment rates were disappointing. Second, if the credit programme was to achieve financial sustainability, it needed to increase significantly the number of its borrowers. It was felt that improvements on either of these fronts could not be achieved without enhancing the technical capacity of SEEDS staff.

Low loan repayment rates were seen to be a direct result of market saturation, and it was felt that an injection of appropriate technical assistance could permit borrowers to graduate into higher-value markets. It was also hoped that this would enable REP to diversify into new areas of economic activity, thus permitting a significant growth in its scale of operations.

Consequently, in 1990 REDS was established with the aim of enhancing the effectiveness and increasing the scale of REP coverage. The initial focus adopted by REDS was that of SEEDS as a whole, namely to work directly with groups of poor people. Its aim was to create employment, particularly in part-time, income-supplementing activities.

This focus has since shifted somewhat. REDS, with extension staff located in each district where SEEDS operates, continues to work with groups – in such activities as the bulk purchase of inputs; linking producer groups directly to market outlets, thus bypassing rent-seeking middlemen; and organizing group storage facilities, which together with credit facilities permit farmers to wait until prices rise after the harvest period. However, its concern with the promotion of sustainable employment and of more productive, higher-income activities has led to a greater emphasis on already established individual producers. This is seen as an effective way of generating growth in rural economies while providing improved skills and sustainable employment for the very poor.

Among the wide range of activities in which REDS is active are goat breeding, various veterinary services, beekeeping, the introduction of improved crop varieties; and a range of artisanal activities, including screen printing, carpentry, coir dust brick manufacture and vehicle repair and welding. Research and development work is undertaken with extensive involvement of small producers themselves. Subsequently, training is provided in the new techniques and credit extended for the purchase of necessary equipment. Other REDS activities include awareness-raising campaigns, demonstrations of specific technologies and ongoing individual business counselling.

An important source of technical information in this work is the international NGO, ITDG, with which REDS has developed a close working relationship. ITDG's international experience has been important in helping REDS to strengthen its capacity on the ground and it remains an important source of specialist advice and input in specific technical areas.

---

[13] Drawn from Jeans and Ruthven (1996).

Impact and cost-effectiveness

The SEEDS programme is growing extremely fast and today reaches 63 700 clients in 1830 villages. Large numbers of clients have benefited from each of REDS' specific project activities. In the period from 1993 to 1996, 10 000 clients received technical training; over 16 000 small businesses received counselling; 6000 farmers were involved in bulk purchases of inputs; and nearly 1500 producers benefited from group marketing schemes. In addition, 285 field demonstrations of agricultural technologies were conducted and a large number of new products and technologies were introduced. This included the launch of 1900 new animal husbandry projects and the adoption of integrated pest management farming methods by 1100 farmers.

A total of 238 small businesses (almost 70 per cent of them run by women) benefited from the adoption of new value-added products and processes as a result of assistance from REDS. An additional 147 enterprises adopted improved technologies and processes to improve traditional and field-based agricultural activities. In addition to these immediate beneficiaries, it can be safely assumed that a large number of other farmers and artisans have copied the new methods from those who received REDS training.

There has been a significant increase in the number of REP clients and the diversity of the loan portfolio, as well as improvements in loan repayment rates. The contribution of REDS to this is confirmed by the fact that it receives from REP 6 per cent of the interest on all loans, as a fee for services.

Until recently, REDS has charged only for training services (though this has been subsidized). However, a recent pilot scheme to test the willingness of its clients to pay for counselling services has shown positive results. Some information services are now paid for. Long-term clients, who had been persuaded of the value of the services provided, have paid for membership of a new REDS business advisory service. This service aims ultimately to recover all costs.

5.2 Training

5.2.1 *Training vouchers scheme for microenterprises, Paraguay[14]*

> Vouchers, which are sold to small producers for around half their total cost, can be used to pay for courses at any of the institutions approved by the government. With decisions on which course to attend left in the hands of the client, there is evidence of improved quality and diversity of courses offered and increased demand for training. Over 11 000 small businesses benefited in the first 20 months of the scheme.

Project description

The Training Voucher Program was initiated by the Ministry of Industry and Commerce (MIC) in Paraguay. The MIC sets the main parameters of the training products to be offered to microenterprises under the scheme (types of skills, subsectors to be covered and so on). It then invites applications from training institutes which can offer these courses for inclusion in the scheme. Approved institutes are then listed in a register of authorized service providers. Announcements are regularly published inviting institutes not participating in the scheme to apply for membership.

Vouchers are sold at a subsidized rate to target group enterprises – they generally pay around 50 per cent of the total cost. They can be used for any course provided by authorized training centres. After the completion of each course, the vouchers are then presented by the training institutes to the MIC for reimbursement.

The scheme benefits from three effective mechanisms to ensure quality control. First, participating training institutes sign a legally binding agreement with the MIC which describes certain features of the services to be provided, including duration, number of hours, subjects to be covered, maximum number of trainees per course and so on. Second, the MIC undertakes periodic, unannounced supervisory visits to all institutes.

Third, and this is perhaps the most interesting and innovative aspect of the scheme, decisions on which institutes will be used,

---

[14] Drawn from Schor and Alberti (1996).

and what type of courses they will teach, lie in the hands of the client microenterprises themselves. If a client is unhappy with a course and consequently does not complete it, the institute gains nothing: participants must attend more than 75 per cent of the classes in any course to enable the institute to claim reimbursement.

In the longer term, since client microentrepreneurs are entitled to 'shop around' in their choice of course, institutes have an incentive to perform well. They rarely make empty promises, not only because their clients would drop out mid-way through courses (depriving them of income), but also because they hope that recommendations from satisfied clients will bring them additional customers.

Impact and cost-effectiveness
In the first 20 months of operation, the programme has enabled 11 324 microentrepreneurs to participate in a total of 696 training courses provided by 61 training institutes. The contribution of the MIC to these courses has been $220,000 (a cost of $19.40 per participant). This is much less than for many more conventional programmes, which have generally stimulated less effective demand and delivered rather less appropriate and relevant skills.

Interestingly, the most popular courses are not the cheapest. The consistent winners in the monthly popularity rankings issued by the scheme are private institutions which focus on the needs of a specific subsector, teaching readily available skills. Popular courses are often taught by practitioners in their workshops. Theoretical courses, often run by state-subsidized institutions, perform worst.

Two current trends offer hope for further successes for the programme. First, microentrepreneurs are exhibiting a growing demand for training. Second, there is evidence of improvements in the quality, appropriateness and diversity of courses on offer as a result of competition between service providers. Consideration is currently being given to integrating the voucher scheme into Paraguay's national training system, using the model for all types of training.

5.3 Technology development and dissemination

5.3.1 *Technoserve – assistance to palm oil processors, Ghana[15]*

> A lack of processing capacity and market outlets in many parts of southern Ghana leads to significant wastage of oil palm fruit. The model developed to address these problems by Technoserve and Ghanaian communities is based on increasing the productivity and capacity of local processors through the establishment of small-scale processing plant at village level. The model has proved highly successful, generating additional employment and proving to be financially sustainable. It is now being replicated elsewhere in the country by the Government of Ghana and the World Bank.

Project description
The sale of palm oil fruit is an important source of income to farmers in southern Ghana. However, due to a lack of fruit processing capacity and market outlets in many areas, wastage levels are often high: in bumper seasons, as much as 40 per cent of the crop rots on the trees.

In 1985, ten farmers in Ntinanko, a small village in Ashanti, set up a co-operative to seek solutions to these problems. The only buyer of palm oil fruit was a nearby large-scale, government-owned palm oil mill. However, the mill suffered from irregular cash flow and vehicle management problems and could not be relied on to buy the farmers' fruit.

The group approached the NGO, Technoserve, for assistance and in 1986 an agreement was signed between them. As an initial step, Technoserve undertook a subsector study in order to gauge the potential for improved productivity and output, and to identify the key bottlenecks that would need to be released to enable this to happen. The study showed that there existed significant demand for palm oil; considerable scope for

---

[15] Drawn from Malhotra and Santer (1994), Bowman (1988) and Hicks and Herne (1997).

increasing local efficiency and productivity through improved management; and potential for increased incomes and employment.

Some of the bottlenecks identified were endemic to virtually all industries in the country at the time, including poor access to credit and necessary inputs, limited managerial capacity and inconsistent tax and import policies. There were, in addition, a number of constraints relating to technology and management specific to the palm oil subsector.

Based on its findings, Technoserve recommended the establishment of a small-scale, labour-intensive palm-oil processing plant and this was commissioned in late 1987. Technoserve also continued its assistance to the group in areas of organization, business management and record-keeping and in the development of a business plan for the processing plant. During this period, group membership increased and was expanded to include local oil-palm processors, all of whom were women. Members made their prescribed equity contributions of 25 per cent of the projected total capital costs, both in cash and in the form of labour and building materials.

For a variety of reasons, the original strategy – to buy fruit locally, process and then sell it – was abandoned after a few months and the group shifted to a 'custom processing' strategy, charging local processors for the use of the plant. Simultaneously, the decision was taken to abandon the screw press, which had proved too small to be commercially viable, in favour of a higher capacity hydraulic press. In addition, Technoserve established a nursery to produce improved seedlings for sale to group members.

Impact and cost-effectiveness
These changes made the difference between success and failure. By the end of the first year of operations, the plant was processing all of the available fruit from the village as well as some from neighbouring villages. The volume of fruit processed by the plant increased from 11 tons in January 1988 to 45 tons in June of the same year, and to an average today of between 60 and 80 tons in the fruiting season. There has been an increase in palm fruit production, including a significant growth in cultivation on land which had previously lain fallow. The number of processors has grown from seven to 55.

The social acceptability of the 'processing services' model established at the plant has been the key to the success of Ntinanko. Rather than displacing traditional processors, it has enhanced their capacity, enabling them to realize as much as tenfold increases in their productivity. These processors have tapped into existing market channels and have developed new market linkages. In addition, the plant has generated employment in porterage and trading. New businesses have been established in the village to provide food, clothing and other services as a result of the increased volume of commercial activities in the village. Financial analysis measured net value-added as a result of the sale of palm oil at $53,700 in the first three years of operation.

The plant has now achieved full autonomy. Full-time management has been transferred to a local manager, who received training from Technoserve. Technological upgrading of the plant has been achieved and a community-owned and -operated oil palm nursery is generating additional funds for community use.

As might be expected, the costs associated with establishing a successful model were high and financial analysis of Ntinanko showed costs exceeding benefits. However, analysis of the first replication of the model found that financial benefits exceeded project costs by a factor of more than five.

The model has been recognized by the Government of Ghana, the World Bank and the Food and Agriculture Organization as a viable and highly desirable model for replication. The Government of Ghana and the World Bank have decided to proceed with the establishment of 23 similar plants in Ghana and Technoserve has been engaged to implement the project.

During the 1996 season, the national palm oil farmers' association's regional chapters started stockpiling palm oil in central locations in order to attract larger industrial buyers, such as soap manufacturers, who pay higher prices for palm oil if they can be assured of purchasing large volumes conveniently. The association is also promoting the development of village-level oil palm nurseries to promote high-yielding, disease-resistant varieties.

5.3.2 Dissemination of the ceramic jiko, Kenya[16]

> By 1989, over 250 000 fuel-efficient stoves (Kenya ceramic jikos or KCJs) had been disseminated in Kenya alone (and since the technology has now become fully commercialized and had spread widely throughout the East Africa region, the numbers are undoubtedly much greater than that today). The project worked from the outset with both artisanal metalworkers and more modern ceramics businesses; and used existing marketing channels.

Project description

In Kenya, practically all of the stoves used up until the early 1980s were of an all-metal design introduced in the early 1900s by Indian labourers and produced by micro-enterprises. While an improvement on the traditional three-stone stoves previously used, they were none the less fuel-inefficient – a progressively more serious problem in a country with a rapidly growing population and shrinking forest areas.

In the early 1980s, the Kenyan NGO, KREDP, with the support of the Ministry of Energy, introduced and modified the Thai Bucket stove. This is a metal stove with a ceramic lining – a key element of fuel-efficient stove design as a result of its insulation capacity. Then, in 1985, USAID approved a three-year grant to the Kenya Energy Non-Government Organizations (KENGO) to complete technical refinements to the stove and to embark on a strategy for its commercial dissemination.

Where it differed from previous, less successful schemes was in its subsectoral approach to the problem. Where earlier initiatives had tended to be somewhat technology-driven, operating from the assumption that once the technical problems were resolved, commercialization would follow naturally, the KENGO approach laid much greater stress on the importance of understanding the 'system' in which artisanal producers operated – including their sources of raw materials, production processes and marketing channels.

This approach gave the project team a much clearer idea than had previously existed both of the range of obstacles in the way of upgrading the quality of jiko production and of the different channels open for the delivery of support to producers. Local master artisans were involved in a programme of technical design work. When the Thai Bucket stove was introduced, these artisans were able to make a key contribution to design adaptations making them more appropriate to production with local raw materials and skills.

However, despite training efforts, local artisanal potters proved unable to produce ceramic liners of the required specifications and quality. At this stage, project managers overcame their initial reservations and chose to involve urban-based, medium-sized companies in the production of the ceramic liners – the received wisdom, after all, was that aid projects should work directly with poor microentrepreneurs. Much of the project's time and resources were spent on helping these producers to move into commercial production of the ceramic liners. The success it achieved in this, as well as in creating linkages between micro- and medium-scale producers, was vital to the ultimate success of the initiative.

While artisanal metalworkers produced the claddings, or the body of the KCJ – generally from scrap materials – their larger partners produced the linings. Having understood from the initial subsector analysis that efficient market channels were already operational in the subsector, the project took a back-seat role in the production and marketing aspects of the KCJ. Much of the credit required by artisans for the production of stove claddings was advanced by their medium-sized partners. And while the government and the project did undertake some general advertising and public awareness campaigns, for the most part artisans were left to exploit existing marketing channels.

---

[16] Drawn from Jeans et al. (1990) and GEMINI (1995b).

Impact and cost-effectiveness

At the outset, the KCJ was priced at around three times the cost of the unimproved metal design. As production levels grew, however, prices soon fell to below half the initial level. While this is still almost double the price of the metal stove ($4 compared with $2.50), the average household recoups its investment in only a few months as a result of fuel savings.

As of 1989, over 250 000 KCJs had been produced in Kenya alone – and the technology has now spread widely in east and southern Africa. Thousands of microentrepreneurs have increased their incomes from the product, for which demand has been particularly strong in fuel-scarce, rapidly-growing urban areas. The technology has also had a favourable environmental impact as the consumption of wood and charcoal has dropped.

The initiative has no further need of outside financial or technical assistance. By working closely with the private sector (both micro- and medium-scale) and exploiting rather than attempting to replace or over-ride already existing channels, the project has been able to stimulate a significant and self-sustaining enhancement of a technology that is of central importance to poor producers and consumers alike.

5.3.3 Treadle pump dissemination, Bangladesh and Senegal[17]

> A fully commercial strategy for the production and dissemination of treadle pumps has yielded major successes in Bangladesh and Senegal. The Bangladesh project has used an extensive network of private traders to achieve nationwide coverage for the technology. The Senegal initiative has used other innovative marketing strategies, including using purchasers in a new area as sales agents, earning a commission on further sales. Both projects have made imaginative use of public awareness campaigns.

Project description

Much of the irrigation equipment introduced into Bangladesh following independence was inappropriate, being too expensive for most farmers, subject to frequent breakdown and difficult to repair. The existing cast-iron drinking-water pumps, on the other hand, required back-breaking work to produce sufficient water for irrigation. In response, two small, manual pumps, whose fully installed cost is between $20 and $50, were introduced in the early 1980s. Financial analysis found that the pumps could generate an annual net return of $100.

The production and dissemination strategy made maximum use of existing private sector channels. Four relatively sophisticated workshops were trained in production of the pumps. A programme of training for village well-drillers was also launched.

The early dissemination strategy employed was to channel pumps through NGOs and other agencies which generally offered generous subsidies. Subsequently, a fully commercial marketing strategy was introduced by the Canadian-based NGO, International Development Enterprises (IDE), based on the removal of all subsidies. This was seen as a prerequisite to total transfer of technology dissemination to the market.

A national mass-marketing campaign was then launched, involving the use of radio, television, cinema, demonstrations at local fairs and village theatre. Training was given to selected artisans nationwide, and a network of authorized traders was established. An IDE logo was placed on pumps that passed inspection. IDE charged a 10 per cent mark-up on the pumps to support project costs and dealers added a 15 per cent margin.

ATI also found that existing irrigation systems were inappropriate for the needs of poor smallholders in the Sahelian zone of Senegal. Its engineers modified one of the small pumps popularized in Bangladesh to make it suitable for local conditions and set about transferring production to the private sector. Beginning in 1991, selected small artisanal businesses were provided with training and follow-up visits over a three month period (initially free, but later for a charge); and tooling (jigs and fixtures). Except for initial sets, all of the tooling was produced by a local medium-scale business, trained and commis-

---

[17] Drawn from Edesess and Pollack (1993) and Hyman (1996).

sioned by the project. The cost of the tooling was recovered through a lease-purchase arrangement.

The project let workshops carve out a local market near their production sites and discouraged competition in the same area if the manufacturer did a good job. By the time the training programme was completed in late 1996, 20 artisans were producing pumps, and these had established themselves into an association, which is already arranging bulk purchases of raw materials at lower unit costs.

The project also provided manufacturers with some training in marketing and all undertook promotional activities, such as producing flyers, displaying pumps at commercial locations and making regular contact with prospective sales agents. In addition, trained artisans were persuaded to designate some early pump purchasers as local representatives, who were paid a commission on sales they generated. By way of sharing the risks of innovation, the project shared the costs of all promotional activities undertaken by artisans for the first year after the completion of training.

The project also undertook a number of promotional activities to popularize the technologies. These included use of television and radio; allowing farmers to borrow pumps for a trial period of one to two months; and negotiating special sales arrangements with several NGOs. In addition, it provided a small credit fund to enable manufacturers to stock raw materials, sell pumps on credit and arrange demonstrations. These loans were administered by the Pump Manufacturers' Association.

Impact and cost-effectiveness
Today, over 700 000 manual irrigation pumps have been installed in Bangladesh, creating $190 million in direct net cash benefits to small farmers over the first seven years of the project: a benefit/cost ratio of more than 40:1. Production and sales of the pumps have moved well beyond the core group trained and authorized by the project. There are now over 75 private pump producers, several thousand well-drillers and around 16 000 dealers selling the pumps.

The much more modest number of pumps disseminated in Senegal – 1750 by early 1997 – can be attributed to the much shorter life of the project and, crucially, to the country's very sparse population. The technology is continuing to spread commercially and the project plans to completely phase out its project activities in late 1997. By the end of 1995, total monetary benefits of the project exceeded total costs by a factor of almost two to one, and this ratio will continue to improve as project costs decline and stop altogether.

ATI is currently seeking to further increase the scale of impact of the project through replication in a number of other countries in West Africa, including Mali, Niger and Nigeria.

5.4 Networking and support to associations

5.4.1 The FIT programme, Kenya[18]

> FIT is promoting the development of networks between small-scale entrepreneurs and other actors with whom they work, including traders and clients. These are facilitating the flow of information on market demand, ideas for product diversification and new sources of equipment. FIT clients have been able to use this information to develop new products and to identify and exploit new markets. Many of the mechanisms developed are sustainable at little cost, and local agencies are showing interest in taking them over.

Project description
FIT is a Dutch-funded programme of the International Labour Office which is implemented in collaboration with the Dutch NGO, TOOL. Its aim is to strengthen local capacity for the development of mechanisms through which non-financial assistance can be provided sustainably to MSEs. Its initial focus is on Kenya and Ghana, in both of which countries it works closely with partner agencies in the design and delivery of a range of innovative services.

---

[18] Drawn from Tanburn (1995, 1996a, 1996b).

This case study describes FIT activities in Kenya. These fall under the following headings, which will be described in turn: rapid market appraisal; user-led innovation workshops; working with traders who service MSEs; enterprise visits and brokering workshops; and the dissemination of written information.

Rapid market appraisal (RMA) RMA methodology was developed in response to a request for assistance by a metalworkers' association in identifying new markets for goods which they might be able to produce. RMA workshops bring together entrepreneurs to develop lists of possible new products through brainstorming and then to identify possible key informants to advise them about these products. Some training is provided in how to approach such people in order to get the best results from the interview. Individuals then go out to make their interviews and come together finally to discuss how to apply what they have learned.

User-led innovation workshops Four workshops, which bring together small-scale producers and groups of their clients, have so far been held. These have brought metalworkers together with farmers, food-processors and transporters. Demand for workshops of this sort, initially at least, have tended to come more from the end-users of MSE products than from the producers themselves. During the workshops, users are given the opportunity to talk about what products they would like to buy.

It became progressively clearer to producers that these workshops were proving to be a valuable source of advice and information. Specifically, the end-users provided information on the likely demand for specific improved or new products and the price and technical specifications which would be acceptable to them. While the users were not prepared to place firm orders, the metalworkers were able to take away ideas and information and to translate them into product innovations.

Working with traders who service MSEs Traders are another potentially important source of information on product innovation that can be undertaken by MSEs. They represent an important window on the world outside that habitually inhabited by artisans. FIT has been sponsoring regular meetings between MSE metalworkers and local traders in Embu. The merchants bring to the meetings products which they buy in Nairobi but which they would source locally if supplies of an appropriate quality were available.

Enterprise visits and brokering workshops Visits to other enterprises offer another important potential source of ideas for innovation among MSEs. This fact is already recognized by the entrepreneurs themselves: an FIT study found that MSEs already organize exchange visits to different parts of the country. FIT's role is to promote this process and towards this end, it has worked with several local NGOs and MSE associations to facilitate enterprise visits and brokering workshops (where MSEs come together to discuss shared problems and ideas), using different formats. The objective in each case is to enable MSEs to exchange information, ideas and contacts and to learn from each other.

Information dissemination Contrary to what has often been believed, FIT has found that MSEs make occasional use of written material and sketches. Various manuals and catalogues were found to be significant sources of information to MSEs which they translated into product innovation. While it is true that few can accurately interpret engineering drawings, photographs and simple sketches can provide inspiration. The pictures in IT Publications' *Tools for Agriculture*, for example, were found to have inspired MSEs to produce new implements. FIT has been exploring how technical information of this type can be made accessible to MSEs on a self-sustaining basis. Approaches identified to date include the use of local street hawkers to sell pamphlets and the production of a newsletter.

Impact and cost-effectiveness
Subsequent monitoring of the impact of the rapid market appraisal (RMA) workshops found that they had a significant impact on the way that participants did business. While

prior to the training, 91 per cent of the sales of participating enterprises had gone through middlemen, subsequently this dropped to 59 per cent as MSEs began to go out to find their own clients. Some 60 per cent of participants increased their sales, while 30 per cent introduced new products as a result. A local consultant who has worked with the scheme has been commissioned to teach it elsewhere in Kenya, and also in Tanzania. The manual has also been translated into Spanish, and is currently being used in Latin America.

Monitoring of the impact of user-led innovation workshops also found positive results: participating MSEs had made and sold agricultural equipment, to new designs developed as a result of the meetings, worth an average of $700 per MSE (although it should be noted that probably only around half of participating enterprises derived significant benefit from the workshops). The value of the workshops to the end-users is reflected in the fact that they are willing to pay all travel costs involved in attending them. Another notable achievement of the meetings has been to involve women farmers in the design process: they made up around 50 per cent of farmers participating in some of the meetings. Meetings are continuing, generally with the facilitation of an agricultural extension agency, and private sector involvement in organizing and facilitating them is currently being explored.

As a result of the FIT-sponsored meetings with traders, orders have been placed with MSEs for a number of products which they had previously not manufactured. These include irrigation equipment, improved agricultural implements and a range of construction-related products, including wheelbarrows and various fixtures. Interestingly, the meetings have also enhanced cohesiveness among the MSEs themselves, who are now moving to buy their raw materials collectively in bulk.

The enterprise visits and brokering workshops have led to the introduction of several new technologies and products. Furthermore, product quality and presentation have both improved noticeably. In subsequent monitoring of MSE visits to large-scale enterprises, 92 per cent of participating entrepreneurs reported gains in self-confidence and expanded horizons. This gain was most noticeable among women entrepreneurs who felt more assertive in their subsequent dealings with employees and customers.

Some 80 per cent of participants on one of the enterprise visits, jointly organized with the NGO, PRIDE, felt that it had helped them to boost their sales by more than 45 per cent. These businesses had on average hired an additional three employees each since the visit. So valuable is this service to MSEs that they are prepared to pay all of the direct costs involved.

An evaluation following one of the brokering workshops found participating businesses to be employing significantly more people than previously. Several MSEs reported that, as a result of the workshop, they had been able to find solutions to problems they had been wrestling with for some time.

An initial exercise in the dissemination of written information involved the printing of booklets containing designs for metalwork equipment. These booklets were priced at $2 to cover all printing and distribution costs and 55 were sold within four weeks. This demonstrates that MSEs are willing to pay for information if it is brought to their place of work. Another initiative, involving a simpler format with the costs of printing and distribution being covered by the sale of advertising, is currently under way. A newsletter, with full costs covered by advertising, is also being considered. No data has yet been collected on the impact of improved availability of written materials. However, the fact that entrepreneurs have been prepared to pay sufficient amounts to cover the full cost of the service indicates that they perceive it to be beneficial.

Much international interest has been shown in the concepts developed by FIT. Projects drawing on its experience are now operative in Uganda and Benin and initiatives in a number of other countries are in the pipeline.

5.4.2 Assistance to small enterprise associations in Ceara State, Brazil[19]

> There has been a transformation in the scale and productivity of small-scale production in Ceara State, Brazil. This has resulted from a two-pronged approach: (1) encouraging state bodies to purchase goods from small producers; and (2) providing technical assistance to enable them to achieve the required standards. With the income of the technical support agency tied to the completion of successful contracts and state agencies under no obligation to buy unless quality standards are achieved, quality of service and of production are guaranteed.

Project description

Assistance by state government agencies in Ceara to small enterprise associations began as part of an emergency employment-generating public works programme in response to a serious drought in 1987–88. The state authorities directed that materials and tools for the works programme be purchased from small producers in the drought-stricken areas. In addition, some customary purchases of goods such as school furniture, grain silos and construction and repair of public buildings were transferred to small enterprises.

Two agencies which had already worked closely in previous small producer support programmes were responsible for the procurement programme – the State Department of Industry and Commerce (SIC) purchased the goods and services, while the Brazilian Small Enterprise Assistance Service (SEBRAE) provided technical assistance to enable their clients to reach the production standards required. The contracting procedure differs in one crucial respect from most other such programmes: if the purchasing state government departments are unhappy with the quality of the goods, they are under no obligation to accept them. This innovation has proved of central importance to the scheme's success.

The scheme works as follows: a state department – such as agriculture, education or health – contracts with the SIC for the provision of goods or services. SIC then makes a contract with SEBRAE to provide necessary technical assistance to small producer associations, paying SEBRAE a 5 per cent commission on the value of completed contracts. SEBRAE in turn contracts with associations – where none exist in specific subsectors, it encourages their formation. SEBRAE advances 50 per cent of the value of the contract to the commissioned association. (This mimics the way that large private concerns habitually subcontract to small producers in Brazil, providing them with substantial working capital for commissioned work.)

A system of product warranties has been established by the scheme. Each item produced carries the name of the producer and if it proves defective, it is returned for repair or replacement. If the producer has closed down in the interim, the association is responsible for all necessary work. The association is also responsible if a particular producer does not deliver on schedule.

These arrangements bring four important factors into play. First, they create a healthy distance between the two sets of government actors – SIC/SEBRAE and the purchasing departments. Second, they make SEBRAE's income dependent on the quality of the work of their clients. Third, by working with associations, the habitual problem of trying to work with many individual enterprises is overcome. And fourth, small producers are encouraged to work closely and co-operatively together: better performing firms have an interest in encouraging laggards to improve the quality of their products.

Impact and cost-effectiveness

The initial impact of the project was sufficiently great that when the drought ended, the programme was continued. In the three-year period from 1989 to 1991, the state government directed $15 million (30 per cent of its total expenditure on goods and services) through the scheme. This gave rise to the expansion or opening of dozens of small brick-making operations, woodwork shops, stone quarries and lime-burners.

---

[19] Drawn from Tendler and Amorim (1996).

In the face of political pressures, the benefits of the scheme have tended in recent years to become dispersed and diluted, as contracts have been spread over the huge area covered by the state. Only in the case of woodworking have efforts been sufficiently concentrated to enable the emergence of a cluster of small producers, permitting a significant leap in their collective efficiency.

At the outset of the scheme, the district of São Joao do Aruaru boasted only four small sawmills, each employing three workers. An initial order for 300 wooden wheelbarrows was met with assistance from SEBRAE. These not only proved more popular than the metal wheelbarrows provided by the previous large-scale producer but also cost 30 per cent less. Within two years, the small-scale woodworkers had successfully met orders for an additional 2000 wheelbarrows, 3000 school desks, 100 tables as well as handles for hoes and backhoes and barrels for the distribution of water. By 1992, they were supplying 40 per cent of the state's needs for school furniture, amounting to 90 000 pieces annually, and had displaced the two large furniture-making plants in southern Brazil.

Five years after the first order for 300 wheelbarrows, the number of sawmills had increased from four to 42, each mill now employing an average of nine permanent workers. An additional four to seven temporary additional workers felled trees, cut them into lumber and transported the lumber to the mills. All in all, this added up to a total of around 1000 people employed directly or indirectly by the mills, more than 10 per cent of the total population of the district. More than half the mills increased their productivity by acquiring powered equipment they did not have before.

The new skills, equipment and confidence that was gained through participation in the programme was used by small producers to break into new private sector markets – furniture for summer homes and hotels – where they have now become permanently ensconced. Indeed, five years after the programme's start, these markets account for 70 per cent of their sales. In addition, an order for 20 000 school desks has also been awarded by a neighbouring state.

Backward and forward linkages to firms in other sectors have developed in almost textbook fashion and with remarkable spontaneity. Local firms moved into the repair and then the production of equipment, initially for sawmilling and then for sugar cane and cassava mills and for cheese-making businesses. A private bus company opened up a local service, five storeowners bought trucks for transporting logs, a new hardwood supplier started operations and the Bank of Brazil opened a branch in the district. The flurry of new manufacturing activity also led to a spurt in housing construction and a new brick-making business opened employing 20 people. The association of woodworkers itself is now an important provider of skills to its members, organizing night schools in co-operation with the local authorities.

Finally, the programme has had a significant impact on the quality of service provided to small producers by SEBRAE. With a vested interest in the performance of its clients, its activities have naturally become more driven by their real needs. Five years after the launch of the initiative, commissions account for 15 per cent of the agency's income.

5.4.3 The Institute of Socio-economic and Technological Research (INSOTEC), Ecuador[20]

> INSOTEC helped the small-scale woodworkers association to establish a supply outlet for raw materials and spare parts, CENTRIMA, with significant financial contributions coming from association members themselves. This has enabled members to get improved access to cheaper supplies, while CENTRIMA has become financially self-sustaining.

Project description
INSOTEC was established in 1980 as an NGO to provide support to small enterprises in Ecuador. Combining the functions of research institute and implementing agency, it provides a number of services including

---
[20] Drawn from Malhotra and Santer (1994).

economic research, design and implementation of technical assistance programmes, technology dissemination and policy and advocacy services.

One of the most distinctive features of INSOTEC's approach is the strong link it maintains with FENAPI, the National Federation of Chambers of Small Industry. Through this link, INSOTEC provides services to various industry associations and then uses them as channels for the delivery of technical assistance, thereby reaching far more small enterprises than would otherwise be possible. Specific assistance to associations includes improving their capacity to conduct regional and subsector studies, management training for staff, and organizing trade fairs.

One of INSOTEC's most successful initiatives to date is its collaboration with the National Association of Small Industry Woodworkers (ANIPIM). In 1989, INSOTEC provided a legal adviser to facilitate the formation of ANIPIM. It then provided advisers to help the new association carry out a subsector analysis of the opportunities and key constraints facing small-scale woodworkers. One of the most pressing problems was found to be the availability, at affordable prices of raw materials – both local lumber and imported items such as equipment, spares, lacquers and varnishes.

As a way of addressing this problem, INSOTEC and ANIPIM jointly conducted an appraisal of the feasibility of establishing a supply outlet, with the former also providing a lawyer to examine different possible legal formats for the outlet. Having decided to proceed, INSOTEC contributed some start-up capital for the establishment of the outlet, called CENTRIMA, and covered the costs of its personnel for the first year.

To date, CENTRIMA has concentrated on the sale of lumber. Besides purchasing inputs for member firms, it has also begun selling to the general public, at slightly higher prices. Its future plans include the direct import of inputs other than wood; the establishment of an information centre to promote new ideas and designs and to encourage quality enhancement; assistance in sourcing and purchasing new capital equipment; and organizing and facilitating members' participation in trade fairs.

Impact and cost-effectiveness

ANIPIM members strongly supported the creation of the supply centre, as demonstrated by their willingness to pledge non-reimbursable funds to support the set-up. Ten members contributed funds for the feasibility study and, subsequently, 22 firms contributed $400 each to capitalize CENTRIMA. INSOTEC attributes much of the subsequent success of the venture to the fact that it was so clearly demand-driven, responding to the articulated needs of ANIPIM members.

Both sales and profits have continued to rise since the establishment of CENTRIMA, surpassing original performance projections. Break-even point was achieved within six months of starting operation. As a result of making bulk purchases, the outlet achieved a 15 per cent discount on plywood and discounts of up to 30 per cent on some other inputs. Products are priced to include a 5 per cent mark-up, which is used to meet operating costs, but the resulting prices still represent substantial savings to small producers relative to the prices they were paying before.

While no enterprise-level impact data exists, sales levels and CENTRIMA profitability indicate that the service provided is highly valued by its clients. It is anticipated that the planned move into the supply of imported items will significantly improve small woodworkers' access to these goods and permit further enhancement in the quality of their produce.

5.4.4 Proyectos de Fomento, Chile[21]

Project description

Proyectos de Fomento, one of the programmes of Chile's official small enterprise support agency, SERCOTEC, was established in 1990 with the aim of promoting clustering and networking between MSEs. The programme is based on a number of assumptions: (1) that one of the principal problems facing MSEs is isolation; (2) that dynamic clusters can have a positive social

---

[21] Drawn from Humphrey and Schmitz (1996).

and economic development on those areas where they are concentrated; and (3) that co-operation between private and public sectors is required if clusters are to be successfully promoted.

There are three stages to the development of programme initiatives (PROFOs) at the local level. First, SERCOTEC establishes contact with a small number of producers active in a specific subsector (usually between 10 and 30) and, following an analysis of their problems and opportunities, seeks agreement with them that a basis for ongoing collaboration exists. A manager is then appointed, with the initial task of acting as an interface between client enterprises and service providers. In this capacity he is able to act as a two-way conduit between local service providers and client enterprises – promoting services and acting as a channel for client feedback.

The manager also facilitates networking and co-operation between client enterprises through exchange visits, group workshops, joint approaches to process and product improvement and so on. The aim of this is to promote collective competitive advantage, so that the economic muscle of individual firms is increased through membership of effective networks within the cluster.

The final element of the PROFO process is the transfer of the initiative to local associations and other institutions. The manager is appointed only for a period of three years. If client enterprises wish to perpetuate the post, they must organize and fund it themselves. The benefits, it is hoped will be sufficient for private initiative alone to sustain it.

Impact and cost-effectiveness

Early results from the PROFO initiative have exceeded SERCOTEC's expectations. Some 16 PROFOs had been established by mid-1993, of which several had already made significant progress in increasing market share, moving into new markets both in Chile and abroad, and in developing subcontracting relationships with large companies. In three cases, groups of small metalworking firms had been able to improve their performance sufficiently to begin supplying the state mining corporation, providing inputs which had previously been imported or manufactured in Santiago.

SERCOTEC was sufficiently encouraged by these results to develop a PROFO programme specifically directed at small firms wishing to enter export markets. Under this initiative, SERCOTEC pays for 70 per cent of the costs of a manager for the first three years and also subsidizes the hiring of consultants to provide specific assistance.

The programme is too young to have generated firm impact or cost-effectiveness data. However, an early evaluation found encouraging results (Dini, 1993) and project managers are optimistic about the possibility of PROFO managers being fully supported by small producer associations.

5.5 Summary

Table 5.1 describes the performance of the case study projects against three key measures of success: benefit–cost ratio, financial sustainability and scale of impact. A lack of data on benefit–cost ratios and on scale of impact is due, in most cases, to the projects being too young to have generated such data. In the case of several older projects, we were unable to identify the relevant data.

The 'financial sustainability' column has been divided into two. The first subcolumn refers to full sustainability, where the benefits of project activities continue to be generated beyond the life of the project. The second denotes that although there continues to be a need for project services, the service-providing institutions or enterprises created by the project have achieved sustainability.

In most cases, the data in Table 5.1 do not do fully reflect the achievements of the projects. This is for three reasons. First, many of the case studies are very recent, with many still being ongoing. Both scale of impact and benefit–cost ratio inevitably grow over time. Similarly, the chances of financial sustainability also improve in the longer-term, particularly when the project is seeking to introduce a technology or service not previously familiar to the target group.

Second, there are strong practical and methodological problems associated with tracking over time the scale of benefits.

Table 5.1 Performance of the case study projects				
		Financially sustainable		
Project	Benefit–cost ratio	Whole operation	Institutions or enterprises created by the project	Scale of impact
BRAC	3:6:1			98 000 household poultry raisers; 750 000 chicks annually; 9000 paravets
Tinytech	Not measured but it can be assumed to be positive		✓	16 250 farmers supply seeds annually; total annual benefits of over $2 million
Alpaca herders			✓	1400 alpaca farmers
REDS				16 000 enterprises received counselling; 10 000 received technical training; 1900 new animal husbandry projects; 1500 benefit from group marketing schemes
Paraguay vouchers				In first 20 months, 11 324 trainees
Ghana oil-millers	5:1:1	✓		4-fold increase in oil processed; 8-fold increase in number of processors; model replicated in 23 other locations
Kenya ceramic jiko project	Not measured but it can be assumed to be positive	✓		By 1989, 250 000 in Kenya alone (wider dissemination has occurred throughout East Africa)
Treadle pumps	40:1 in Bangladesh; 2:1 in Senegal (but growing in this recent project)	✓		Bangladesh – 700 000 pumps; Senegal – 1750 pumps
FIT			Several of the mechanisms continuing without project support	
Ceara State	Not measured but it can be assumed to be positive			In woodworking sector alone: 1000 new jobs and substantial stimulation of local economy
INSOTEC			✓	
PROFOs			Not yet proven but grounds for optimism	

Measuring the scale of outreach of the KCJ or treadle pump projects, for example, where production techniques are disseminating without any further involvement of the project is difficult and costly.

Third, there are also methodological problems involved in measuring the *depth* of benefits accruing from initiatives such as those described here.[22] As we have seen in the case studies, an enhancement in the capacity and productivity of the target group frequently provokes a wider increase in economic activity. This can take the form of strengthened backward or forward linkages: that is, increased demand for goods and services by producers who enjoy increased earnings; or the increased capacity of producers to provide improved equipment, inputs and

---

[22] These problems are resolvable, and we will return to the question of appropriate impact assessment systems in the final chapter. It none the less remains true that most of the case studies have attempted to capture and quantify few of their wider downstream benefits.

services for other economic actors, permitting wider productivity gains.

Measurements of the wider benefits accruing from specific interventions have been made. Studies in Sub-Saharan Africa, for example, indicate that each additional dollar of income from agriculture adds $2–$3 to the overall economy (Pinstrup-Andersen et al. 1995). None the less, they are both complex and expensive to achieve and have not been undertaken in any of the above evaluations.

Despite these shortcomings, the data in Table 5.1 represent significant achievements in terms of both scale of impact and cost-effectiveness. In the next chapter, we will attempt to disentangle the various factors underlying these achievements.

6 Factors underlying high impact and cost-effectiveness in service delivery to small producers

The case studies provide a good overview of many of the more interesting recent innovations in the field. They represent a significant step forward from the conventional and much maligned image of the business development service project. Moreover, they throw up many interesting ideas and approaches which hold out the promise of further advances.

Three things, above all, immediately stand out. First, *there are solid achievements in terms* of developmental impact. These include employment-generation, increased incomes, foreign exchange earnings and local economic regeneration.

Second, *these achievements could not have been made on the basis of a minimalist approach.* The range of constraints faced by small producers – in, for example, the poultry-raising sector in Bangladesh or in the production and processing of alpaca fibre in Bolivia to name but two of the most obvious cases – was such that improved access to credit alone (or to any other single input for that matter) would not have permitted these results.

Third, under certain circumstances, the benefits generated by business development services can significantly outweigh their costs.

Before going on to identify the factors underlying these achievements, however, let us once again acknowledge the limitations of the data presented in the previous chapter. Many of the findings are somewhat provisional in nature: a number of the projects described are ongoing and several are so young as not yet to have generated solid impact data. Moreover, they represent a huge variety of project activities covering many different types of services, target groups and geographical conditions. This makes comparisons and generalizations difficult.

These are significant limitations. Let us not forget, however, that our objective here is not to reach definitive conclusions about best practice in the design and delivery of business development services or about the conditions under which a 'credit plus' approach will yield optimal results. We have recognized from the outset that the impact assessment data necessary for such a task is not available. Our aim, rather is, in the short term, to challenge conventional wisdom and to stimulate discussion; and, in the longer term, to promote a deeper and more thorough investigation of the key issues raised.

So what then of the core themes to emerge from the case studies? In spite of their heterogeneity, certain clear patterns are none the less discernible. Four are particularly interesting from our perspective:

- achievement of scale of operations;
- greater role of market mechanisms;
- facilitative role of the state; and
- enhanced exposure of small producers to the outside world

6.1 Achievement of scale of operations

The achievement of scale is one of the key elements underlying the success in recent years of minimalist credit programmes. Conventionally, it has been assumed that such economies of scale are rarely if ever open to the providers of business development services: while the financial packages appropriate to the needs of the poor are relatively limited in number and standard in design, most business development services, it is assumed, need to be tailored to the needs of more specific target groups.

In a sense, this remains true. The ability of many business development services to be carefully targeted so as to reach producers with specific problems or market opportunities has already been noted. None the less, the case studies reveal a number of different ways in which such targeting is compatible with wide scale of outreach. The most important of these, which will be addressed below, are the following:

- the use of a subsector approach;
- directing assistance towards key subsectoral nodal points where goods and services affecting many small producers pass through a small number of hands;
- promotion of subcontracting; and
- promotion of project replication.

6.1.1 Subsector approach

The use of a subsector approach to the analysis and diagnosis of small producer constraints and the design of appropriate interventions is shared by almost all of the case studies presented above. In short, this approach requires that the focus of study – and of intervention – be not the individual small producer, but the system (or subsector) in which he operates (Boomgard et al., 1992; Malhotra and Santer, 1994; Lusby, 1995).

Subsector analysis involves a study of the vertical structure of a given economic activity – such as blacksmithing, silk production or dry-season gardening – from input supply through production process and marketing of the finished product. This permits the identification of: (1) bottlenecks constraining the economic activity; (2) niches in which small producers can have a comparative advantage; and (3) specific interventions which can ease the bottlenecks and facilitate the exploitation of niche opportunities.

There are three key differences between this approach and those conventionally employed. First, whereas conventional studies of the 'informal sector' identify problems shared by small producers and recommend broad, non-specific interventions, subsector analysis permits the identification of problems – and solutions – that are specific to the system within which small producers actually operate. This is no more than common sense: conditions relating to, for example, raw materials' availability, potential for technological upgrading and market opportunities are necessarily subsector-specific.

Second, the perspective of the small producer is recognized as being only one of a number within the subsector that are worthy of attention. Thus, for example, the producer's view that credit access is the core problem needs to be set within the context of analyses of trends in subsector demand, access to improved technology, availability of raw materials and so on.

Third, it permits a more dynamic and flexible approach to small producer support. With the operating environment of small producers seen in systemic terms, it is much easier to build into the design of interventions capacity to adapt to new conditions and challenges emerging as a result of project achievements. A World Bank report found this to be an 'extremely successful' innovation:

> The minimalist approach consists of adopting a narrow and modest focus, such as on credit only. The process approach consists of gradually broadening the scope of a programme to remove one bottleneck at a time, according to the priorities identified by participants. (Dessing, 1990)

Subsector analysis permits the identification of systemic interventions that can benefit large numbers of small producers at the same time at two different levels:

- changes in policy and the elimination of restrictive practices and regulations that constrain the activities of large numbers of producers; and
- interventions addressed towards system nodes – key actors such as intermediary organizations, suppliers and distributors – where many products or services pass through a small number of hands.

Interventions at the policy level offer substantial scope for leverage (that is, of generating benefits significantly greater that the scale or cost of the intervention). A few examples will serve to illustrate this point. The removal of an import tariff on sewing machines, formerly taxed as a luxury good, had a major impact on small-scale tailors in Sierra Leone. Similarly, the approval given by the Government of Ghana and various international development agencies for donor funds to be used for the import of high quality, second-hand engineering equipment led to a significant enhancement in the technological capacity of small machine shops (that would otherwise not have been affordable), with wide downstream benefits for the large number of individuals and companies that they service (Smillie, 1991; Dawson, 1991).

Conversely, an unconducive policy environment can inhibit the scope for small producer development. Bhalla and Reddy (1994), for example, describe how the cheap prices set for petrol and diesel discourage the adoption of small-scale, renewable energy (or biogas) technologies in India.

One final policy area in which significant leverage at subsectoral level can be achieved is through the sourcing of goods and services required by local government departments from small producers. As noted in the previous chapter, this has stimulated a transformation in the scale and quality of small-scale production among woodworkers in Ceara State, Brazil.

6.1.2 Working through subsectoral nodal points

There are a number of nodal points, where products and services which have the potential to benefit large numbers of small producers pass through a relatively small number of hands. The point for service providers when directing assistance towards nodal points is to be clear about the distinction between 'beneficiaries' and 'target groups'. It may be entirely appropriate and legitimate for an initiative seeking to reach a particular category of *beneficiaries* to direct some (or all) of its efforts towards a quite different *target group* – if that group is considered to be the most effective channel for the widespread delivery of services to the beneficiaries.

The most important nodal points to feature in the case studies are strategically placed enterprises such as tool and equipment manufacturers; traders and retailers; and sectoral associations and clusters.

Strategically placed enterprises, which are often relatively large and sophisticated, can be highly effective and commercially sustainable channels for the delivery of assistance to small producers. This was evident in two of the case studies: assistance provided to modern ceramics companies in Kenya permitted the development of the fuel-efficient KCJ; while the delivery of the Tinytech oil mills to relatively large-scale entrepreneurs stimulated significant rural activity, with strong benefits accruing to small producers in many sectors of rural Zimbabwe.

A number of other recent initiatives further reinforce the point. Helping large concerns to adopt prawn-rearing acquaculture technology opened up supplies of larvae to hundreds of small producers in central Java (Gamser, 1988). Training provided by ITDG to modern small enterprises in Zimbabwe in the production of manually-operated wheel-making equipment enabled artisanal producers all over the country to manufacture their own wheels, thus addressing a major constraint in the production of ox-carts and other rural vehicles (ITDG, 1995a).

Several large-scale manufacturing firms in Thailand were taught to produce an improved reeler, which then became available to hundreds of small silk producers, permitting them to significantly improve their productivity and capacity (GEMINI, 1995b). Finally, the Central Java Enterprise Development Project successfully promoted increased production and incomes of hundreds of rural furniture makers by helping a single export firm seek out new international markets for Indonesian rattan furniture (Boomgard, 1988).

Strategically placed enterprises capable of extending benefits widely are not always large and sophisticated. Village blacksmiths and barefoot vets, for example, act as important disseminators of equipment and services to many.

Traders and retailers also represent an important subsectoral nodal point, capable of influencing large numbers of small producers. Small producer support projects are demonstrating much greater willingness than previously in making use of private distributors for the sustainable dissemination of small producer products. The mass outreach of treadle pumps in Bangladesh, for example, was based on the stimulation of existing market channels and the establishment of a nationwide network of authorized dealers. Similarly, the success of the KCJ dissemination strategy and of the Ghana palm oil milling project were based on exploiting existing private trading networks.

The FIT project has sought to stimulate and strengthen private market channels for the dissemination of MSE products. Meetings with traders have proved to be an important source of information for its client MSEs: a number of new products have been introduced as a result and wider markets have been opened up. A number of other recent projects – including, for example, the Senegal treadle pump project and ITDG's Rural Stoves West Kenya project (ITDG, 1995b) – have also sought to actively involve traders in their commercial dissemination strategies.

Small producer associations and clusters offer obvious scope for support agencies to reach many clients with limited activities. Large numbers of producers in both the Brazilian and Chilean clusters described in the case studies have derived significant benefits from services delivered through their respective associations. Similarly, the supply outlet CENTRIMA in Ecuador has increased the availability and reduced the cost of raw materials supplied to large numbers of members of the woodworkers association, ANIPIM.

Many small-scale metalworkers and fitters clustered in an informal industrial area of Kumasi, Ghana were also found to enjoy significant benefits as a result of the technology development work undertaken with a small number of engineering workshops in their midst. An enhancement in the capacity of the machine shops – which enabled them to improve the range and quality of equipment and components they provided to the less sophisticated majority of MSEs – was found to have had a significant beneficial impact on the collective efficiency of the entire cluster (Dawson, 1991; Smillie, 1991).

Our understanding of why some clusters become dynamic and innovative growth poles while others experience little qualitative upgrading remains limited. One recent review found three important factors which appear to be shared by many successful clusters (Humphrey and Schmitz, 1996). First, they are driven primarily by the needs of clients, particularly those in export markets, rather than by supply-side efforts to stimulate their capabilities. A second and related factor is the presence within the cluster of marketing agents, providing ideas from and potential access to non-local markets.

Third, the presence of specialist support agencies providing services relevant to the needs of firms within the dominant subsectors appears to be a near universal condition of successful clusters. This is confirmed by another overview study into small enterprise clusters in Latin America (Spath, 1993). The activities of the Technology Consultancy Centre were found to be among the key factors in explaining the dynamism of the cluster in Kumasi, Ghana (Dawson, 1991).

Where specialist support agencies are less prevalent, associations can play a leading role in service delivery. In the leather sector in Colombia, for example, a dynamic industry association, ASECUEROS, offers a wide variety of courses, sponsors technical consultants and encourages networking and information-sharing among firms. Half of the 34 sampled small and medium-sized leather-working enterprises in a World Bank study were found to have received technical assistance from ASECUEROS (Levy et al., 1994).

The role of clusters and small producer associations has been considerably more important to date in Asia and Latin America than in Africa. In part this is attributable to differences in population density: the generally thin population in Africa has inhibited the development of clusters, of mass markets for them to serve, and of potential economies of scale on the part of service providers. In addition, there is little tradition of associations in much of Africa and they tend to be institutionally weak.

None the less, the experience of the Kumasi cluster and of several efforts at strengthening African small producer associations in recent years offers hope for further advances. We will return to this theme in the last chapter.

6.1.3 Promotion of subcontracting and state procurement

Despite the fact that subcontracting and state procurement have not yet proved to be as important an engine of small producer growth as had once been hoped, they do none the less remain a potential source of leveraged intervention. The case of the woodworking cluster in Ceara, Brazil demonstrates the depth and breadth of impact that can be achieved through an appropriate mix of technical assistance and opening up of market channels to large-scale clients.

The potential of subcontracting in stimulating small producer growth was underlined by a recent World Bank study of successful small enterprise support systems in four countries – Colombia, Indonesia, Korea and Japan (Levy et al., 1994). It found linkages with large firms to be an important source of information and market access for small producers in many sectors.

The problems in developing such linkages to the large-scale private sector and the state are legion and well documented: these include limited access among small producers to the necessary working capital, equipment and skills; and frequent delays in payment by state agencies, further exacerbating working capital problems. These problems are particularly great in Africa. A recent study in Kenya found that: 'there are strong forces working against local sub-contracting. ... Given the levels of education and skills, the transaction costs and risks are high. An efficient system for sub-contracting requires large markets and low transaction costs. Kenya is not there yet' (quoted in Tanburn, 1996b).

None the less, some progress is being made in this field. The Small and Medium Enterprise Initiative, recently launched jointly by the South African corporations Anglo-American Corporation and de Beers with the intention of providing assistance to prospective small-scale subcontractors, has enjoyed some encouraging early results and a number of goods and services have been successfully subcontracted out (O'Dowd, 1997).

6.1.4 Promotion of programme replication

Most of the case studies have proactive strategies for project replication – including the preparation of manuals, training materials and various cross-country linkages. Furthermore, there is considerable evidence of success towards this goal. The experience of projects such as the Ghana oil-milling project and the Ceara cluster indicate that governments and major multilateral donor agencies are also becoming more involved in this field. In a number of cases – the treadle pump and KCJ initiatives, for example – private sector replication is already occurring, with the production techniques spreading spontaneously between producers.

It remains unquestionably true that few business development services will be capable of transfer to other social and economic environments with the facility generally enjoyed by credit programmes. None the less, the case studies suggest that there exists considerably more scope than has often been thought.

6.2 Greater role of market mechanisms

A second major area of innovation is a much greater use than previously of market mechanisms both for the delivery of project services and the dissemination of the benefits that they generate. In the face of the shrinking of the state as a result of structural adjustment and greater emphasis in project initiatives on enterprise development (as opposed to more welfare-oriented notions of 'income generation'), business development service projects have increasingly turned to the private sector.

Four specific developments are evident:

- using and strengthening existing private sector production and marketing channels rather than seeking to over-ride them;
- promoting competition between the providers of business development services;
- aiming at full financial sustainability for the institutions created by projects; and
- obliging client small producers to pay at least a portion of the cost of services.

6.2.1 Using existing production and marketing channels

There has been a strong trend in recent years for projects to work with small producers from the outset, in the selection, adaptation and commercialization of new techniques and technologies. This is in contrast with conventional approaches which too often saw 'expert' engineers do much of this work in isolation.

Nowhere is the shift to working with existing private sector productive capacity better illustrated than in the readiness of projects to turn to larger and more modern enterprises to supply technologies or components where small producers prove unable to make them – Tinytech oil mills, ceramic liners for the KCJs, wheel-making equipment and so on. In each of these cases, the project designers overcame initial resistance to working with larger enterprises in order to address constraints facing their small producer clients.

A similar process (as noted above) is evident in the greater use that projects now make of existing market mechanisms, including private traders, often seen by NGOs as a rapacious middleman whose role projects needed to subvert. Project use of market channels to promote small producers today extends to the Internet. The NGO, PEOPLink has recently set up an Electronic Catalogue and a Global Gallery to sell the products of partner agencies internationally. E-mail and the Web are proving cheap and effective means for the rapid exchange of information (on design, availability, prices and so on) between producers in the South and prospective clients in the North (Velzeboer, 1996). These are markets in which speed and ease of communications are of the essence.

One final development of note in this field is the adoption by small producers, usually through their associations, of warranty systems. The absence of such systems has often discouraged formal sector buyers from sourcing goods from small producers. The value of an effective warranty system, and the capacity of clients to reject substandard goods, were among the key reasons for the success of the Ceara initiative. Warranties and seals of approval are being increasingly used as a way of inspiring trust in the goods and services of small producers.

6.2.2 Promoting competition between the providers of business development services

A number of projects are currently experimenting with different ways of creating market conditions for service provision. One is to encourage direct competition between agencies providing similar services. The Paraguay training voucher scheme is a mechanism that could be applied to any field of activity in which more than one service provider is active in a given area.

A second idea currently being explored is to tie the earnings of the provider to the performance of its clients. The incentives offered in this manner to SEBRAE were seen to be an important factor in its provision of high-quality technical assistance to small producers in Ceara State, Brazil. Similarly, the commission earned by the service-provider on sales of treadle pumps in Bangladesh encouraged it to maximize the scale of dissemination.

One interesting development evident in a number of the case studies, as a result of greater commercialization of service delivery, is the larger role now being played by small producers themselves in the provision of training. Some of the most popular courses offered under the Paraguay voucher scheme are offered by small producers in their workshops. This is a sure sign of training becoming more truly driven by the demand of its clients.

6.2.3 Aiming at full financial sustainability for the institutions created by projects

As donors have come to lay a higher premium on financial sustainability, so business development service providers have sought ways of ensuring that benefits continue beyond the life of projects without need for further subsidy.

In some cases, this has been achieved by transferring the production of new technologies entirely to the private sector, as with the KCJs and treadle pumps. In other cases, however, support institutions need to be created and achieving financial sustainability for these is generally more difficult. One route, favoured by the American NGO, ATI, is to identify services that might be capable of commercialization and establishing a for-profit company for these, leaving non-commercializable services with a sister NGO. Thus, CORPOCA, the alpaca processing and marketing facility is well on the way to full financial sustainability. A similar route was followed by the woodworking producer association ANIPIM whose raw material supply depot CENTRIMA is now a profitable business.

The Chilean PROFOs have adopted a 'pump-priming' strategy, whereby the project pays for the costs of a manager for a limited period of time. Only if client small producers value the service to the point of being willing to pay for it after this period will it continue. ITDG's service centres in Zimbabwe are following a similar route. These centres hire out engineering equipment to small producers, enabling them to significantly improve the quality and extend the range of products. To continue beyond the initial period of subsidized support, however, the centres must generate sufficient business to become fully cost-recovering. The prospects of this occurring in the case of both initiatives currently appear good.

ITDG Kenya's Decentralized Animal Health (DAH) Unit is also seeking full financial self-sustainability. Its aim is to promote the use of low-cost veterinary approaches in East Africa through training, research and the development of monitoring and evaluation systems, and it has already undertaken a number of contracts on behalf of governments, donors and other agencies in the region. A target of three years for full commercialization has been set and the Unit is exploring the possibility of finding an institutional home inside a Kenyan agency.

6.2.4 Small producers pay for services

There are now few business development service projects which do not require a financial contribution from its clients towards the cost of services – a far cry from the situation prevailing only a few years ago. The size of the contribution varies, according primarily to the type of service provided and the level of poverty experienced by the target group. Few agencies, for example, expect to recover all costs involved in providing training or counselling.

Nor are client financial contributions restricted to payment for service delivery. In several of the case studies – the Ghana oil-milling project and the CENTRIMA supply centre in Ecuador – clients also made substantial contributions to the start-up costs of the initiative.

6.3 Facilitative role of the state

In parallel with increased exposure to market mechanisms, the case studies point to a diminished – *though by no means insignificant* – role for the state in small producer promotion. In only one of the case studies – support to the Ceara clusters – is the state the principal service provider. And even here, the technical assistance agency, SEBRAE, operates in many respects as a private sector operator.

The aim here is *not* to argue that the state has no role to play in the delivery of services to small producers. There are cases where it is the only likely provider or where, indeed, it may well have a comparative advantage over other agencies. The point, rather, is to observe the emerging trend for the state to play a greater role in establishing an environment conducive for small producer development and, thereafter, playing a largely 'hands-off', facilitative role.

Mention has already been made above of the ability of governments to achieve significant leverage through both policy interventions and the sourcing of goods and services from small producers. The local authorities in Ceara also played a crucial role in establishing the legal framework, including the warranty system, that was essential to the scheme's success. Similarly, we have seen (in the case of the Paraguay voucher scheme) the potential for government to encourage competition between service providers as well as establishing the conditions – authorizing and supervising training agencies – necessary for its success.

One final, important role of the state to emerge from the case studies is in facilitating dissemination of small-scale technologies. This can be done in one of two ways: first, by funding the replication of successful models, as in the case of the Technoserve-supported oil-milling plants in Ghana. Second, by participation in public awareness campaigns. This can take the form of promoting specific goods, such as stoves or treadle pumps. Or it can involve promoting small producers more generally through trade fairs and the like. The Governments of Kenya and Ghana have both been active in this latter field.

6.4 Enhanced exposure of small producers to the outside world

One final core trend to emerge from the case studies is the importance which support agencies attach to increasing the exposure of their clients to non-local markets. We quoted Smillie above, referring to the limitations of a minimalist credit programme in Kenya in the following terms: 'Women borrowers assuredly make the best of their loans, but their endeavours are limited to the narrow confines of the world to which they are generally restricted' (Smillie, 1991). Among service providers seeking to promote innovation in cost-effective ways, addressing this constraint has assumed an increasing prominence in recent years.

The importance of uncodified knowledge – expertise that develops informally, through visits to other producers, via the movement of individuals from one enterprise to another, and so on – to the process of innovation is widely recognized (Tanburn, 1996a). Preparatory work undertaken by the FIT programme in Kenya suggests that small producers themselves are aware of the importance of external sources of information. Some of those interviewed organized group visits to producers in other parts of the country. Furthermore, clients – and particularly those asking for new types of products – were valued as sources of information and ideas: one small enterprise in Kenya was found to have formed a focus group of people representing its target market (Daniels, 1996). Traders were also found to be an important source of information to producers in FIT's preparatory studies. Some 60 per cent of sampled traders had given small-scale metalworkers specific design orders (ibid.).

Until recently, few initiatives have attempted to build on these informal structures and to improve the access of small producers to information networks in a systematic way. The results of recent attempts to use and strengthen information networking – with a view to increasing capacity for uncodified knowledge acquisition – suggest that this may be an area with significant potential for further cost-effective, high-leverage interventions.

In a number of the case studies, projects have facilitated the participation of clients in trade fairs. FIT has found firm evidence that 'exhibitors in MSE exhibitions derive much benefit from seeing the exhibits of their competitors; as a result they are inspired with new product ideas, which they subsequently try to manufacture' (Esbin, 1994). The potential of small producer trade fairs to stimulate innovation is underlined by Humphrey and Schmitz (1996) in their review of the emergence of dynamic clusters in developing countries:

> Particularly where clusters are dormant, trade fairs can have a catalytic effect: the fair provides a clear indication of what customers want and how rival enterprises are meeting the customers' needs. Once some producers respond to these needs and receive new orders, those who do not will try harder. The transparency of the process induces a sense of rivalry among local producers, of laggards imitating leaders, of leaders having to search for further innovations. Trade fairs, that is the extreme concentration in time and space of producers and buyers, can have such a jump-start effect.

Similarly, on the basis of ongoing research on small-scale industry in Indonesia, Sandee (1994) suggests that in attempts to stimulate and upgrade rudimentary clusters, the most effective first step may be to take local producers to relevant fairs and markets before injecting training, technical or financial assistance.

Trade fairs are only the most visible of a whole range of activities evident in the case studies aimed at promoting exposure for small producers to non-local markets. The FIT programme has been particularly active in this area. Its various activities – rapid market appraisal; group meetings of producers and end-users; meetings between producers and traders; enterprise visits and brokering workshops; and the dissemination of technical information – are based on the premise that one of the primary constraints facing small producers is isolation: isolation, that is, from information on new markets, new product ideas, new technologies and new sources of supply. The encouraging results achieved by this project and the low cost of many of the activities suggest that this approach is worth further exploration.

6.5 Summary

The case studies presented in Chapter 5 offer evidence of high impact and cost-effectiveness in a variety of business development service programmes for small producers, some of which also involve the delivery of credit. While caution must be exercised in the interpretation of some of the performance data, drawn as it is from programmes that are mostly still relatively young, sufficient evidence of strong achievement is available to warrant guarded optimism.

Of particular interest, in seeking to understand the factors underlying this success, is the apparent adoption – and adaptation – by business development service providers of several of the key principles of minimalist credit: an increasing use of commercial approaches; and breakthroughs in achieving scale of operations through leveraged interventions. The emergence of subsector approaches has been of particular importance in this regard.

It would, however, be wrong to suppose that the challenges offered by the delivery of financial and non-financial services are essentially the same. On the evidence of our case studies, the gulf between them may not be as wide as has often been supposed, and there appears to be scope for the transfer between them of certain underlying principles. But in a number of important respects they differ; and these differences have important implications, particularly in terms of how they are to be funded in the long term.

As programmes become more demand-driven and market-channelled, the scope for cost-recovery increases. Moreover, there is solid evidence that some types of business development service may well be financially sustainable. None the less, there are good reasons for believing that certain core activities will continue to need some level of long-term subsidy. While much can be achieved by strengthening the positive trends evident in business development service provision, and in increasing synergies between credit and non-credit interventions, sight should not be lost of the fact that the market is unlikely to be able to deliver all of the required services. These questions will be the subject of the final chapter.

7 The way forward

So, where do we go from here? The evidence presented here suggests that the time is ripe for a shift in the orientation and balance of programmes of support to small producers. The strong focus in recent years on the need for *institutional* sustainability among support agencies has meant that questions relating to the sustainability of the *impact* of interventions on small producers have been somewhat neglected. It is time for the re-establishment of a proper balance between these two concerns.

There is ample evidence that business development service providers have understood the need for a reorientation of their working methods. The array of experiments in both market-driven, demand-responsive services and revenue-generating activities bear testimony to this. The challenge now is for governments, and particularly the donor community, to meet the challenge presented.

As we have seen, significant progress has been made in recent years in the design and delivery of business development services. Much work, none the less, remains to be done, and it is here that the initiators and funders of support programmes now have a key role to play. The case studies map out the terrain to be explored. However, experiments are, for the most part, still in their infancy. While early results are most encouraging, more seed capital for further experimentation is required.

This chapter will address five broad areas where attention needs to be directed. These will be discussed in turn.

- maximizing synergies between financial and business development services;
- building on recent market-driven developments;
- improving impact monitoring and assessment;
- developing strategies for those areas where the market mechanisms are less effective; and
- re-examining questions of sustainability and subsidy.

7.1 Maximizing synergies between financial and business development services

Central to the argument in this paper is that there are significant potential synergies between financial and business development services. Several of the case studies suggest various ways in which these might be realized. The experience of REDS, for example, provides evidence that the provision of complementary technical services can have the effect of increasing both the coverage and the repayment rates of credit schemes, thus effectively promoting innovation and growth among small producers. Several of the other initiatives, most notably the BRAC assistance to poultry raisers and the Bolivian alpaca project, give clues as to how credit can be judicially used to unblock bottlenecks in what are essentially technical support projects.

Our understanding of the complementarities between financial and non-financial services, and how they can most effectively be realized, none the less, remains weak. One result of the trend towards minimalism in recent years is that few credit projects are aware of the potential benefits of working closely with technical support service providers; while few technical agencies know how to address the financial constraints faced by their clients.

There is substantial scope for a move towards a more complementary approach, without a return to large, inefficient organizations attempting to deliver many services at the same time. Further research into best practice in this field is required, leading to the production of guidelines, both for the designers of projects and for practitioners involved in their implementation.

7.2 Building on recent market-driven developments

The case studies themselves give ample coverage of the range of specific interesting innovations in the field, and it is not necessary here to cover that ground again. The aim, rather, is to point out several key areas where further research could yield significant results.

7.2.1 Share the risks of innovation

There are substantial risks involved in the development, production and marketing of new products by small producers. These risks accrue to the producers themselves (will the product be commercially viable?); to commercial distributors (will there be a market for the product?); and to end-users (will the product be reliable, repairable, and/or appropriate?). By sharing the risks with these actors, support agencies can play an important role, often at little cost, in facilitating the development of the small producer sector.

The case studies suggest various ways in which risks can be shared. The development of warranty systems and seals of approval, for example, represents an important breakthrough in making traders and end-users less vulnerable to the risk of buying faulty goods. Further refinements to and dissemination of warranty systems are important if local government agencies and the formal sector are to become significant clients for small producers.

In the FIT project in Kenya, several entrepreneurs wanted to develop new products in response to ideas that had been proposed in meetings with farmers. The farmers, however, were unwilling to place orders, being unsure of the ability of the MSEs to produce goods of an acceptable standard. With no deposits for commissioned goods, MSEs had neither the necessary working capital nor a guaranteed market. FIT made available a small fund for raw materials (which gave grants of $20–$30 to selected enterprises), and this led to the successful development of a number of new MSE products. This approach 'shared the risk'; the MSEs contributed their time and energy, and consumables to the process. The seed capital yielded high returns: sales resulting directly from the innovations resulting from this fund amounted to an average of $780 per enterprise (Tanburn, 1996a).

Scope exists for further experimentation with risk-sharing. Small investments, in the form of 'seed capital' to encourage the production or dissemination of small producer goods, can achieve significant leverage. Moreover, if agreements can be made between client and provider on the recoupment of fees in cases of successful innovation, there is no reason why such schemes should not be financially self-sustaining.

7.2.2 Promote the acquisition of uncodified knowledge

The importance of informal channels for the acquisition of skills and knowledge among small producers has already been discussed at length above. This whole area appears to hold significant potential, not least because of the low cost involved in establishing and strengthening these channels. Facilitating meetings between various subsector actors, participation of small producers at trade fairs, the distribution of appropriate written information are both inexpensive and relatively easy for local agencies to take over if they prove to be of value.

The work undertaken by FIT in this field should be seen as a bold first step. Much more work, none the less, remains to be done. Research needs to be focused on: (1) identifying which activities are capable of commercialization, under what conditions and how this might best be achieved; and (2) measuring the wider developmental impacts of different approaches.

7.2.3 Experiment with clusters and associations

As we have seen, clusters and producer associations offer substantial scope for leveraged interventions. On the one hand, the development of vertical linkages and the presence of key market actors – suppliers, traders, equipment manufacturers and maintenance facilities – can substantially increase the 'collective efficiency' of the cluster. On the other hand, the geographical concentration of producers permits both careful targeting of services and the achievement of scale. Important breakthroughs have been made by clusters in Latin

America, and to some degree in Asia, and our understanding of the elements that go to make up innovative and dynamic clusters is increasing (Humphrey and Schmitz, 1996).

It is, none the less, true that clusters tend to 'happen' spontaneously rather than as a result of planning. Tendler and Amorim's (1996) description of the development of the woodworking cluster in Ceara noted that it received much less official support than another one which failed to develop. The moral to be drawn is not that planners should not interfere, but rather that our understanding of how the process can be facilitated needs to be improved.

Particular attention needs to be focused on the situation in Africa, where neither clusters nor associations have been as successful as elsewhere. While there are a number of factors specific to Africa (described in the previous chapter) that would appear to inhibit their development, much that is transferable can be learned from the Latin American and Asian experiences.

7.2.4 Put decisions on service provision into the hands of the clients

The Paraguay voucher scheme demonstrates the potential dividends to be had from shifting the emphasis on service provision from the provider to the client. There is no apparent reason why such a scheme could not be more widely replicated, not just geographically, but also in terms of the services provided. In any situation where there is potential for competition between several providers of a service, the issuing of vouchers and of lists of approved agencies has the potential to effect a significant improvement in the quality of service.

7.2.5 Make the revenue of support agencies dependent on the performance of their clients

Another way to stimulate an improvement in the delivery of genuinely demand-driven services is to tie the revenue of the provider to the performance of its clients. In the case of Ceara state, Brazil, this proved to be a strong incentive for SEBRAE, the technical assistance agency. While this is easier to do in areas such as Ceara, where a commission can be taken on large, visible contracts, other less formal possibilities also exist.

Contracts with small producer associations, for example, could contain provision for a certain proportion of net income gains – to either individual producers or the association itself – to be diverted to the service provider. This would probably work only where the association had an ongoing incentive to retain links with the provider or where a relationship of trust had developed between them.

Currently, many support agencies have little real incentive to see a significant improvement in the performance of their clients. These two strategies – transferring decisions on services into the hands of the users and tying the revenue of support agencies to the performance of their clients – may contribute to the establishment of a genuine partnership between providers and small producers, with strong potential benefits for both.

7.3 Improving impact monitoring and assessment

There is an increasing awareness among business development service providers of the importance of rigorous impact monitoring and assessment – as tools both for project management and for identifying the factors underlying project failures and successes. However, resources for this are currently inadequate.

Specifically, there is a need for the development of methodologies which are appropriate to the scale and nature of business development service projects. To a much greater degree than for financial programmes, benefits are difficult to capture, being widely dispersed between the immediate target groups and the various downstream beneficiaries to which they provide goods and services.

A solid start has been made to address some of these problems. Haggblade, for example, has outlined a low-cost methodology for simple analysis of the costs and benefits of small producer projects (1991). However, insufficient attention has been paid to experimenting with this or other approaches, with practitioners complaining of insufficient funding. If we are to develop a true understanding of the developmental impact of differing types of small producer support, more resources need to be made available for the development and implementation of appropriate monitoring and assessment methodologies.

7.4 Developing strategies for those areas where the market mechanisms are less effective

The market has a strong and growing role to play in the delivery of services to small producers. None the less, we should not lose sight of the fact that there will always be areas – both geographical, sectoral and in terms of services – in which market mechanisms are unlikely to be so effective. In poor isolated regions (such as large parts of rural Africa) which have only limited involvement in the monetized economy, for example, the scope for market delivery of services has obvious limits.

Similarly, the scope for full cost-recovery for certain services needs to be set against the fact that in a number of core areas – including the design and development of technologies and many types of training – this is most unlikely to be possible. In addition, while increased attention to project replication holds out considerable promise for a further widening of the scale of benefits, the development and demonstration of the original concepts to be replicated will continue to need funding.

Activities in certain sectors are also more likely than others to need assistance that cannot be provided directly through the market. The light engineering sector, for example, plays a key role in the process of indigenous technological learning and is of huge strategic significance. The capacity to develop and adapt equipment (rather than to be dependent on outside sources) is an essential step in the process of social and economic development. Moreover, it is a field of activity that is largely scale-neutral: there is little that a large machine shop could do that, given access to necessary capital and skills, could not be done just as well at a small scale. There is, indeed, some evidence that smallness of scale in this field may offer certain advantages in terms of flexibility of production systems (Schmitz, 1992; Dawson, 1992).

However, in terms of both the cost of the equipment, the level of skills training required and necessary technology development work, it is relatively expensive. While the medium- and long-term benefits of investment in this field can be substantial, they cannot be realized in the short term. Furthermore, problems of cost-recovery are further compounded by the fact that beneficiaries extend well beyond the immediate (generally rather small) target group. Activities of this sort can be considered as building the foundations of an indigenous technological capacity, foundations on which producers in many other sectors will build. These are rarely amenable to purely market-driven approaches.

In short, the conclusion is unavoidable that in certain cases, questions relating to how we define sustainability as well as the place of subsidy in small producer support will need to be re-examined.

7.5 Re-examining questions of sustainability and subsidy

The way in which we use the term 'sustainability' when referring to development projects has undergone a subtle, but highly significant shift in recent years. Conventionally, discussions on the subject of sustainability related primarily to the *impact* of interventions on project clients or beneficiaries: the concern was whether they could sustain the advances achieved as a result of the project once it had ended.

Today, by contrast, sustainability is generally used to refer to the capacity of a project to become self-sustaining, to recover its costs – in other words, *institutional* sustainability. It is in this context that the popularity of minimalist credit must be understood: one of its primary attractions to project funders is the scope it offers for full cost-recovery.

However, in the light of the limitations of minimalist credit described above, the time has come to re-examine the relative importance we attach to financial and developmental sustainability. There are indications that this may be already happening:

As the fundamental analysis of credit programmes shifts from the emphasis on the banker's perspective ('did they repay the loan') to emphasis on the development perspective ('did they need the loan?, did it help them?') the single-minded commitment to credit is being reconsidered. (Grierson, 1994)

This process needs to be taken forward. Adherence to strict criteria of institutional sustainability will rule out many of the types of services that could stimulate the development of small producers. Moreover, it will be particularly the poor, being least connected to markets, who will lose out most.

In short, there is a place for subsidy in small producer support. Much care needs to be given to how and when it is appropriate: the concerns expressed by donor agencies at the prospect of entering funding commitments where there is no obvious exit strategy are quite reasonable. Two guiding principles are suggested here as to how the use of subsidies can be mediated, at least to some degree, by project performance and cost-effectiveness.

The first is that questions surrounding institutional sustainability should be applied to the bodies *created* by projects rather than to the projects themselves. Let us draw some examples from the case studies to illustrate this. Several of the actors described – the input supplier, CENTRIMA; the Tinytech oil mills; the oil processing plant established with Technoserve assistance in Ghana; the CORPOCA alpaca facility – have the potential to become fully cost-recovering initiatives (in fact, several of these are already self-sustaining).

However, neither the specific projects nor the agencies which provided the services necessary for these achievements – such as, in the above cases, ITDG, ATI and Technoserve – can hope to be fully cost-recovering. This fact should be accepted by donor agencies. While it is important that all actors in the field of small producer support operate as cost-effectively as possible, there is a case for requiring differing criteria for measuring the sustainability of, on the one hand, projects and umbrella support agencies and, on the other, the bodies on the ground that they work with.

Second, the prime (but not only) consideration when considering funding proposals should be a comparison of costs and global benefits. While questions of cost-recovery are unquestionably important, there are cases where the benefits are so widely dispersed that revenue collection necessarily proves extremely difficult for the support agency. Moreover, this is particularly true in strategically important areas, such as the light engineering sector, where the enhanced capacity of assisted producers brings widespread benefits elsewhere in the economy.

This brings us back to the issue of impact assessment, and underscores the need for the development of methodologies to capture the downstream benefits of many business development services. If the scale of such benefits is seen to outweigh the costs of specific project interventions, there is a strong case for supporting them, regardless of the institutional sustainability of the service provider.

Selective subsidy has been part of the experience of all developed and newly industrialized countries. Provided that previous abuses are avoided, and that recent developments in demand-driven service delivery can be built on, selective subsidy should be seen as a tool in the policy maker's armoury rather than an evil to be avoided.

7.6 Conclusion

These are interesting times in the field of small producer support. The challenge to business development service providers to achieve scale and cost-effectiveness has been met with imagination, and promising approaches have proliferated in recent years. This has coincided with emerging evidence of the limited developmental impact of minimalist credit.

A new paradigm for small producer support, building on the best to emerge from innovations in both credit and business development services, and exploiting the synergies between them, is emerging. Liberalization and market fragmentation offer unprecedented opportunities to small producers. The task now is to build the support structures which will permit their exploitation.

The case studies presented here offer interesting and innovative ideas on what such structures might look like and how they might operate. They provide the foundations on which further action research must be built.

Bibliography

ATI, Catalyst:, *ATI Bulletin No. 25*, Washington, 1994

Bagachwa, M.S.D., 'The Impact of Adjustment Policies on the Small Enterprise Sector in Tanzania', in B. Helmsing (ed.), *Small Enterprise Development in a Changing Policy Environment: Structural Adjustment and Direct Assistance Programmes in Africa*, IT Publications, London, 1991

Barnett, A., 'Technology and Small-scale Production', *Small Enterprise Development*, Vol. 6, No. 4, IT Publications, 1995

Berger, M., 'Giving Women Credit: The Strengths and Limitations of Credit as a Tool for Alleviating Poverty', in *World Development 17 (7)*, 1989

Berger, M. and M. Buvinic (eds), *Womens' Ventures: Assistance to the Informal Sector in Latin America*, Kumarian Press, 1989

Bhalla, A.S. and A.K.N. Reddy, *The Technological Transformation of Rural India*, IT Publications, 1994

Biggs, T., M. Shah and P. Srivastava, *Technological Capabilities in African Enterprises*, World Bank Technical Paper No. 288, Washington, 1995

Boomgard, James J., 'Developing Small Business in Central Java: Reflections on the CJEDP Experiment', Washington, DC: Development Alternatives Inc., 1988

Boomgard, J.J., S.P. Davies and S.J. Haggblade, 'A Subsector Approach to Small Enterprise Promotion and Research', *World Development*, Vol. 20, No. 2, pp 199–212, 1992

Bowman, M., 'Cost-Effectiveness: Measuring the Impact of Training and Technical Assistance' in SEEP, *Technical Assistance and Training: What Difference Does it Make? How Can it be Done Effectively and Affordably?*, New York, 1988

Buvinic, M., M. Berger and C. Jaramillo, 'Impact of a Credit Project for Women and Men Microentrepreneurs in Quito, Equador', in *Women's Ventures: Assistance to the Informal Sector in Latin America*, M. Berger and M. Buvinic, Kumarian Press, Boulder, 1989

Chen, M. (ed.), *Beyond Credit: A Subsector Approach to Promoting Women's Enterprises*, Aga Khan Foundation Canada, Ottowa, 1996

Creevey, L.E., K. Ndour and A. Thaim, *Evaluation of the Impacts of PRIDE/VITA*, GEMINI Technical Report 94, Washington, 1995

Daniels, A., *The Product Development Process: Identification of a Framework for Positive Intervention*, APT Enterprise Development, UK, 1996

Daniels, L., D.C. Mead and M. Musinga, *Employment and Income in Micro and Small Enterprises in Kenya: Results of a 1995 Survey*, K-REP Research Paper 26, Nairobi, 1995

Dawson, J., 'The Development of Small-Scale Industry in Ghana: A Case Study of Kumasi', in H. Thomas et al. (eds), *Small-Scale Strategies for Industrial Restructuring*, IT Publications, 1991

Dawson, J., 'The Relevance of the Flexible Specialization Paradigm for Small-scale Industrial Restructuring in Ghana', *IDS Bulletin*, Vol. 23, No. 3, 1992

Dawson, J., 'The Impact of Structural Adjustment on the Small Enterprise Sector: A Comparison of the Ghanaian and Tanzanian Experiences', in Helmsing et al., *Small Enterprise Development in a Changing Policy Environment: Structural Adjustment and Direct Assistance Programmes in Africa*, IT Publications, London, 1993

Dawson, J. and B. Oyeyinka, *Structural Adjustment and the Urban Informal Sector in* Nigeria, World Employment Programme Research Working Paper 65, ILO, Geneva, 1993

Dessing, M., *Support for Microenterprises: Lessons for Sub-Saharan Africa*, World Bank Technical Paper 122, Washington, 1990

Dini, M., *Los Proyectos de Fomento*, SERCOTEC, Santiago, 1993

Esbin, H. *Marketing Channels for MSEs in Kenya: Analysis and Strategic Plan*, FIT Working Document No. 5, Nairobi, 1994

Everett, J. and M. Savara, 'Institutional Credit as a Strategy Towards Self-Reliance for Petty Commodity Producers in India', in H. Afshar (ed.), *Women, Development and Survival in the Third World*, Longman, London, 1991

Fluitman, F. (ed.), *Training for Work in the Informal Sector*, ILO Geneva, 1989

Gamser, M., *Power from the People: User Involvement in Energy Technology and Innovation*, IT Publications, London, 1988

Gamser, M. and F. Almond, 'The Role of Technology in Microenterprise Development', in J. Levitsky (ed.), *Microenterprises in Developing Countries*, IT Publications, London, 1990

GEMINI, *Non-Financial Assistance to Small Business Entrepreneurs*, Microenterprise Development Brief No. 5, GEMINI, Washington, 1995a

GEMINI, *Providing Cost-Effective, Indirect Assistance to Microenterprises*, Microenterprise Development Brief No. 16, GEMINI, Washington, 1995b

Goetz, A. and R. Sen Gupta, 'Who Takes the Credit?: Gender, Power and Control over Loan Use in Rural Credit Programmes', IDS Working Paper No.8, Brighton, 1994

Goldmark, L., *Business Development Services: A Framework for Analysis*, Inter-American Development Bank, 1996

Grierson, J., *A Review of ODA's Small Enterprise Development Activities*, ODA, London, 1994

Guzman, M.M. and M.C. Castro, 'From a Woman's Guarantee Fund to a Bank for Microenterprise: Process and Results', in M. Berger and M. Buvinic, *Women's Ventures: Assistance to the Informal Sector in Latin America*, Kumarian Press, Boulder, 1989

Haggblade, S., *The Hang Glider: A Minimalist Proposal for Monitoring Small Enterprise Promotion*, GEMINI, Washington, 1991

Haggblade, S., *Promoting Rural Industrial Linkages Within Agrarian Economies for Rural Poverty Alleviation*, UNIDO, 1995

Harper, M., 'The Programme for the Development of Small Enterprises (DESAP) of the Carvajal Foundation in Cali, Colombia', in F. Fluitman (ed.), *Training for Work in the Informal Sector*, ILO Geneva, 1989

Hicks, F. and J. Herne, 'Small-scale oil-milling in Ghana', *Small Enterprise development Journal*, Vol. 8, No. 3, IT Publications, September 1997

Holt, S. and H. Ribe, *Developing Financial Institutions for the Poor: Reducing Gender Barriers (Draft)*, World Bank, 1990

Hulme, D. and P. Mosley, *Finance Against Poverty*, Routledge, London, 1996

Humphrey, J. and H. Schmitz, 'The Triple C Approach to Local Industrial Policy', in *World Development*, Vol. 24, No. 12, 1996

Hyman, E., *How NGOs Can Accelerate the Commercialization of Agricultural Technology in Africa*, ATI, 1996

Hyman, E., L. Stoch and V. Budinich, *1995 Report on ATI's Program Impact and Learning*, Washington, 1996

ITDG, *Manufacture and Diffusion of Low-cost Transport Devices in Zimbabwe: Phase 4 Final Impact Assessment and Evaluation*, Rugby, 1995a

ITDG, *Evaluation of the Rural Stoves Western Kenya (RSWK) Project*, Rugby, 1995b

Jeans, A. and O. Ruthven, *Sarvodya: REDS Project Completion Report 1993-96*, ODA Joint Funding Scheme, London, 1996

Jeans, A., E. Hyman and M. O'Donnell, *Technology – The Key to Increasing the Productivity* of Microenterprises, GEMINI Working Paper No. 8, Washington, 1990

Johnson, S. and B. Rogaly, *Microfinance and Poverty Reduction*, Oxfam, Oxford, 1997

Khander, S.R. and B. Khalily, *The Bangladesh Rural Advancement Committee's Credit Programmes: Performance and Sustainability*, World Bank Discussion Paper 324, Washington, 1996

Levy, B., A. Berry, M. Itoh, L. Kim, J. Nugent and S. Urata, *Technical and Marketing Support Systems for Successful Small and Medium-Sized Enterprises in Four Countries*, World Bank Policy Research Working Paper 1400, Washington, 1994

Little, I.M.D., D. Mazumdar and J. Page Jr., *Small Manufacturing Enterprises: A Comparative Analysis of India and Other Economies*, Oxford University Press, 1987

Lusby F., *The Subsector/Trade Group Method: A Demand-driven Approach to Nonfinancial Assistance for Micro and Small Enterprises*, GEMINI Working Paper 55, Washington, 1995

McVay, M., *Non-Financial Services for Microenterprises: A Situation Assessment (Draft)*, CARE, Atlanta, 1996

Mayoux, L., *From Vicious to Virtuous Circles: Gender and Microenterprise Development*, UNRISD, Geneva, 1995

Malhotra, M. and J. Santer, *Towards More Cost-effective Nonfinancial Assistance: Case Studies in Subsector-based MSE Development*, GEMINI Working Paper 49, Washington, 1994

Mead, D., T. Dichter, Y. Fisseha and S. Haggblade, *Prospects for Enhancing the Performance of Micro and Small-scale Nonfarm Enterprises in Niger*, GEMINI, Washington, 1990

Meagher, K. and M.B. Yunusa, *Coping with Structural Adjustment in the Informal Sector in Nigeria*, UNRISD, Geneva, 1994

MkNelly, B. and C. Dunford, *Are Credit and Savings Effective Against Hunger and Malnutrition? A Literature Review and Analysis*, Freedom From Hunger Research Paper No. 1, 1996

Montgomery, R., D. Bhattacharya and D. Hulme, 'Credit for the Poor in Bangladesh: The BRAC Rural Development Programme and the Government Thana Resource Development and Employment Programme', in D. Hulme and P. Mosley (eds), *Finance Against Poverty Vol II*, London 1996

Noponen, H. 'Organising Women Petty Traders and Home-based Producers: A Case of Working Women's Forum, India', in Menefee Singh A. and A. Kelles-Viitanen (eds), *Invisible Hands: Women in Home-based Production*, Sage, London, 1987

O'Dowd, M., *Linking Big and Small*, Anglo-American Corporation, South Africa, 1997

Osmani, S., 'Limits to the alleviation of poverty through non-farm credits', *Journal of the Bangladesh Institute of Development Studies*, 18 (4), 1989

Pinstrup-Andersen, P., M. Lundberg and J. Garrett, *Foreign Assistance to Agriculture: A Win–win Proposition*, Food Policy Report, IFPRI, Washington DC, 1995

Pratt, V., *Mobilizing Large Business to Support Small Enterprises: The K-MAP Experience in Kenya*, Paper presented to the Enterprise Forum '96, ILO, Geneva, 1996

Rogaly B., 'Micro-finance Evangelism, 'Destitute Women', and the Hard Selling of a New Anti-Poverty Formula', in *Development in Practice*, Vol 6, No.2, 1996

Rutherford, S., *ASA: The Biography of an NGO, Empowerment and Credit in Rural Bangladesh*, Association for Social Advancement, Dhaka, 1995

Sandee, H., 'The Impact of Technological Change on Inter-firm Linkages: A Case Study of Clustered Small-scale Roof Tile Enterprises in Central Java', in P.O. Pedersen, A. Sverisson et al. (eds), *Flexible Specialization: The Dynamics of Small-scale Industry in the South*, IT Publications, 1994

Schmitz, H., 'Small Firms and Flexible Specialization in Developing Countries', in *Labour and Society*, Vol. 15, No. 3, 1992

www.ingramcontent.com/pod-product-compliance
Ingram Content Group UK Ltd.
Pitfield, Milton Keynes, MK11 3LW, UK
UKHW050227150426
5217IPUK00023B/1676